Transformational
LEADERSHIP

*How To Lead
From Your Strengths And
Maximize Your Impact*

Dr. Richard K. Nongard

Transformational Leadership:
How To Lead From Your Strengths And Maximize Your Impact

Dr. Richard K. Nongard

ISBN: 978-1-312-14340-1

Edited by James Hazlerig

Cover graphics by Dustin Tilly-Sturgeon

First Printing: June 2014

PeachTree Professional Education, Inc.

7107 S. Yale, Ste 370
Tulsa, OK 74136
(918) 236-6116

www.FastCEUs.com

www.Leadership-Certification.com

About the Author

Dr. Richard Nongard is a licensed marriage and family therapist with a Master's Degree in Counseling from Liberty University and a Doctorate in Transformational Leadership (Cultural Transformation) from Bakke Graduate University.

He has written a number of different textbooks for mental health professionals. His most recent book, *Contextual Psychology: Integrating Mindfulness-Based Approaches Into Effective Therapy* has been a best seller among healthcare leaders.

He is a coach, consultant and lecturer, offering services to business groups, ministries and healthcare organizations. In the past, his work has included both inpatient and outpatient psychiatric and substance abuse settings, where he's worked with a wide variety of clients over the years.

His studies in leadership include participating in Christian community development and as the Executive Director of one of nation's largest continuing education companies for mental health professionals. He is also the Chief Strategy Director at Bakke Graduate University, guiding the University through significant change in the marketplace of Christian higher education.

You can bring Dr. Richard K. Nongard to your organization to train your executives or front line employees in Transformational Leadership, Appreciative Inquiry and/or Multiple Intelligences.

Contact Dr. Richard K. Nongard at www.FastCEUs.com or (918) 236-6116

FOREWORD

By Gwen Dewey

Bakke Graduate University (BGU) is about transformation—of ourselves, each other, and the world in which we live. Our faculty and student body include urban leaders from around the world who have become integrated into an international network of leaders in diverse fields, such as urban studies, Christian theology, and ethical business. Richard K. Nongard is one of these transformational leaders.

Richard K. Nongard completed his Doctor of Transformational Leadership (DTL) degree at BGU in June 2013. Prior to his entering BGU, like many of our students, he was already a very successful practitioner. Richard, a Licensed Marriage and Family Therapist and CEO of a successful business delivering Continuing Education Units for mental health professionals, was already a sought-after keynote and conference speaker.

Richard entered the Doctorate of Transformational Leadership program at BGU to more fully research and understand transformational leadership. I have had the privilege of working closely with Richard while he was still a doctoral student and following his graduation in 2013 in his capacity as Chief Strategy Director of BGU.

Richard's new book, *Transformational Leadership: How To Lead From Your Strengths And Maximize Your Impact,* grew out of his dissertation. However, what makes this book so powerful are the additive qualities Richard brings to this subject. In this book, Richard builds upon research in transformational leadership and then adds value by integrating all of his previous learning, experience, and stories from years of experience as a licensed therapist.

In its few pages, Richard shares with the reader the essence of Transformational Leadership and builds on this by sharing with the reader practical ways to generate self-awareness, develop their own personal leadership, improve self-management, enhance emotional and social intelligence in a leadership role, find their calling, be a great mentor, and communicate effectively as a leader.

Following Richard's guidance, you will learn how you can lead from your strengths to maximize your input and create lasting change. Richard's goal in this book is to provide you, the reader, the foundation for making true change in your world, within your community, and within yourself.

Richard believes that everyone, not just CEO's, can be transformational leaders and realize their potential and impact their world. This book focuses on not "when you become a leader", but on you, the reader "as a leader" and stimulates you to utilize the God-given gifts within yourself.

I believe you will find, as I have, that this book is a repository of all kinds of practical ways, specific examples and methods, and timely wisdom that will enable you to understand the processes involved in transformational leadership; you will begin to see yourself as a transformational leader in fresh new ways. You will find yourself returning often to this book as you use it as your handbook for creating permanent change as a transformational leader.

Gwen Dewey, Ed.D., D.Min.
Past-President
Bakke Graduate University
Seattle, Washington
April 2014

Gwen Dewey, Ed.D., D.Min. has a doctorate from the University of Washington in educational policy, governance, and administration, and a Doctor of Ministry from Eastern Baptist theological Seminary in transformational leadership for the global church. She was past President of Bakke Graduate University and teaches in the U.S. and globally. She has experience both in the corporate world and in education, holding key administrative positions at each level. She served as professor in the graduate educational administration program at Pacific Lutheran University, Tacoma, Washington.

Contents

Chapter One

Everything I Know About Leadership, I Learned In Therapy

Almost every leadership book that I've read focuses on historical models of leadership. From Moses in the Old Testament to recent figures like Nelson Mandela—leaders of nations. Almost every business leadership book that I read focuses on the CEO, whether that's Steve Jobs or Jack Welch or any other rock star CEO. Simply put, leadership is often viewed in a limited context. Leadership is seen as something for people of status.

The truth is that most of us are never going to lead a multinational corporation or be the president of a powerful country, but that's not what leadership is about for a vast majority of people.

As a therapist, I had the job of leading one person at a time to important change. As a therapist, I had to confront my own neurotic tendencies to be an effective guide for others. This is the heart of Transformational Leadership: to transform others while transforming one's self.

Why is transformation necessary? The simple answer is this: because nothing stays the same. Transformational Leadership is important not because something needs to change, but because things are always changing. Transformational Leadership is the natural state of life, both in business and on an individual level.

One of my most recent clients in therapy was a diabetic who had just experienced an amputation. Because he continued to smoke after the amputation, oxygen was not reaching the extremities of his body, and he was not healing. The reason he called my office was to get help with smoking cessation.

My intervention with this client didn't draw from my toolbox of psychological therapies, but rather from my toolbox in Transformational Leadership, because our goal was to help him to make a lasting change. Of course, we started with the knowledge that change is inevitable; but we wanted to choose what kind of change he would experience while making sure the change would last. It's through this lens that I was able to create change where previously it had been resisted. Transformational Leadership helped me walk with him into a new chapter of his life, a chapter of life that I had entered when I quit smoking more than a decade ago.

This type of leadership is far more common than the leadership on which most textbooks and training programs focus. It's far more likely that you will lead a small group of families through difficult times as a pastor or as a family therapist than to be the pastor of a mega-church or the next Virginia Satir. You are far more likely to use your creative capacity in business as a small entrepreneur, supervising two to three associates, than you are to be the CEO of a big-box retailer. In management, you're far more likely to be responsible for the performance of individual employees than you are to be responsible for the 305,000 worldwide employees of General Electric. You are far more likely to both need and develop leadership skills at an intimate level than in the paradigms written about in most leadership training manuals.

A lot of leadership books ask you to think about what it would be like in the future when you are a leader. Instead, I invite you to take a moment right now as you read this material and think about how you can fulfill the role of a leader in the community where you are right now. In order to become an effective Transformational Leader, you need to recognize that you are actually already a Transformational Leader. The important question to answer is this:

How can you fully realize your potential and become an even more potent leader within your family, within your community, within your business organizations, within your nation, and even within the world?

Transformational Leadership at its core is about being with people. It's not about doing something *to* people, but doing something *with* them. As a therapist, I learned that leadership is collaborative. As a therapist, I learned the value of just sitting with somebody, of just being with them. It has been said that good therapy is "bellybutton to bellybutton communication," and this metaphor describes therapy as an exchange where both client and therapist are nurtured and grow. Effective leadership ultimately strengthens both the leader and those being led.

Before my doctorate from Bakke Graduate University, much of what I had learned about leadership had come from my practice and counseling clients one-on-one. The knowledge in leadership was fortified by my academic studies and in my dissertation. But counseling aids in the process of change, and that the role of the therapist is to guide a person through this transformation. In some cases this transformation is based on elective decision, but in many cases, the change is inevitable: Counseling is sought to make the inevitable transition tolerable. This is also true in organizational leadership, educational leadership, healthcare leadership, community leadership (in both large and small organizations).

I look back on my many years as a therapist and ask myself: What did I learn about leadership in therapy? I recognize that it taught me many things about Transformational Leadership:

Transformation is the norm in life. Absolutely nothing stays the same.

The issue is not how to change, but how to transform while change occurs.

Leadership is not just for the CEO or international politician—a concept all of us must understand in order to improve our connections to others, even on a one-on-one level.

A leader (or therapist) must be willing to make his own changes in order to be effective in provoking change in others.

Leadership is about making tomorrow better than today. I have collaborated with my therapy clients to help them acquire a new vision that inspires them to make change. We've collaborated to help them create a growth mindset that's based on progress rather than perfection.

Leadership involves inspiring others to employ creativity, which is the key to original solutions and positive growth.

Leadership is a personal journey: One of my most profound insights as a therapist was that therapy transformed me.

My clients caused me to challenge myself, my own thinking, and my actions. I learned that I need to find my own search for significance and new skills at every level. To effectively lead people through transformation, I needed to transform. I am not now the same person that I was at the outset of this process. My theoretical orientation has changed; my relationship to spiritual thought has changed. And I've become not only more effective, but happier, more accepting, and more effective as a counselor.

I went into the therapy field before managed care became the norm. Over the last 25 years, the significant changes in the economics of counseling have brought changes to the way therapy is structured and how services are provided. Because that change was inevitable, my own transformation was necessary. And Transformational Leadership has been the key that's helped me, my clients, and my own business and community experience success.

In addition to being a therapist, I've served as a teacher; I've also served as president of an international professional association. I've seen many inevitable changes in the delivery of healthcare services, as well as legislative changes and a variety of shifting organizational needs. All of this has required personal transformation, which was only possible when I recognized that internal transformation and change were prerequisites to being an effective leader for others.

Whenever I talk about making personal change, people think I'm talking about the things they need to stop doing. Well, perhaps there are some things that are holding you back from your greatest level of potential, but chances are, for you to be an effective leader, the real question is this: *How do I start using those internal strengths and resources which I already possess?*

In this book, we are going to explore the ideas of Transformational Leadership. But more importantly, this book is designed to be a how-to manual. It will teach you how to transform yourself while transforming others--whether your calling is to be an executive, a small business entrepreneur, a local pastor, a therapist, or a person who simply wants the world to be a better place. It is not required that you either are or aspire to be a worldwide political leader, a CEO, or a famous philanthropist. This book is about exceptional, yet everyday, leadership.

For those who implement the ideas contained in this book, the outcomes will be profound. I know that you're going to experience success. You'll not only gain followers as you lead, but you'll even find your own pathway to intuitively solve problems and find good even in situations where others lack hope. The process this book is going to guide you through can make you accepting, adaptable, and giving—while at the same time enhancing your personal power and enlarging the impact of your influence on others.

Do you want to experience success in every level of your life? Do you want to be a more effective pastor, executive, counselor, or entrepreneur? Transformational Leadership is paradoxical. You will learn how to help others while helping yourself. And you will learn that through processes unique to those who maximize their leadership potential, you can make the world a better place.

While we are going to take a look at some of both the academic and the popular definitions of various forms of leadership in this book, sometimes it's easier to define a concept like leadership through example. So before we go any further, let me share with you two examples of leadership.

At the 2014 Consumer Electronics show in Las Vegas, the CEO of T-Mobile, John Ledger, made a speech. Instead of wearing a suit and tie, he came out wearing a T-shirt and sneakers, holding a can of Red Bull. He actually gave a speech that was filled with mild profanity. This led to him being nicknamed "The Rebel CEO."

In the United States, our telecommunications companies actually are years behind the telecommunications companies in both Asia and Europe, as well as other parts of the world. Ledger's goal is to transform the American telecommunications industry. The jury is certainly out as to whether or not his leadership style or, more accurately, his personal style reflected in his leadership, is going to be an effective vehicle for leading T-Mobile into the future.

Nonetheless, some of the things that he has done over the past year have been transformational. So far during his short tenure as CEO of T-Mobile, he has challenged the price structure of the American telecommunications industry. He has altered relationships in supplier partnerships and distribution networks, and he's challenged the status quo of all telecommunications companies, forcing other companies to respond to him. This is pretty remarkable considering the other players in the telecommunications are actually bigger than T-Mobile. But T-Mobile, at least at the current time, seems to be leading us into the future in American telecommunications.

While his tenure at T-Mobile may be short or long, or whether it's viewed as effective or not, John Ledger is such a unique leader in the corporate world that his model of leadership will be something that's discussed for some time. I imagine somebody will even write a book about him and about his leadership style. Future writers will look back at his years at T-Mobile and evaluate whether or not it was a pivotal moment necessary to lead the company into the future. Some will undoubtedly love John Ledger, thinking he's an incredible Transformational Leader. And because he's a polarizing figure, there will be others who will think that his performance was less than stellar. Nonetheless, people will be talking about him and T-Mobile for some time to come.

Now at the same he was talking at the Consumer Electronics Show in Las Vegas in 2014, I was actually having dinner with a friend of mine at a local Vegas restaurant. There were a few of us there: a physician friend, a friend who works at the front desk of one of the larger hotels in Las Vegas, and another friend who actually manages one of the local health and gym studios. As I was talking to my friend who works at the front desk in one of the larger hotels, I was telling her about my project and putting this book together on leadership. And as we were talking about the impact one person can have on another person, she told me a story. A story she hadn't identified as being about leadership, but one that I thought was a perfect example of effective leadership.

Over the past Christmas holiday with 84 team members on her team at her hotel, she knew that somebody would be alone for the holidays, that somebody on her team would not get a card, that somebody on her team of 84 people would feel lonely or unloved. So what she did was pretty remarkable. She actually used her day off from work to create 84 handmade Christmas cards for her employees. She came in early for work one day, before her shift began, and she put all her cards in the employees mailboxes, wishing all on her team a Merry Christmas. She is not the team leader; she is not a department manager; she is not the president of the company. She is a front line employee like the other 84 employees on her team. But what she did through compassion and caring was as powerful as any of the decisions that the CEO can make.

John Ledger is a CEO; my friend is a hotel front desk clerk. Both of them have the capacity to impact people's lives in a positive and meaningful way. Transformational Leadership is for all of us, and it's for you as well.

As you participate in this book and read to the various chapters, I'd like for you to be asking yourself at the conclusion of each chapter:

> *What's one thing that I can take from today's chapter and apply*
> *to my own experience and my own life so that I can be a more*
> *effective leader where I am called to serve?*

As you read this book, perhaps you're a CEO, and you are thinking to yourself:

What decision can I implement that would transform our company?

Or perhaps you're like me and you're a therapist. So when the next client walks through your door, the question for you would be:

How can I lead this person to a lasting change, which can assist this person in resolving the difficulties that, to this point, they've been unable to resolve?

Perhaps you're a small business person and your business to this point has been successful but you'd like to take it to the next level—maybe even cross that million dollar mark in annual sales or create a program within your small company to have a positive impact on the community in an act of Social Entrepreneurship. Different people will read this book for a variety of different reasons, but my hope is that in each of the various sections of this book, you'll be able to take something with you that could help you be an effective Transformational Leader.

How do you define Transformational Leadership?

I'm going to start with a pop culture definition of Transformational Leadership, from Wikipedia. Of course, Wikipedia is not a source for academic writing, but as a reflection of popular definitions, it can be a starting point for us to understand the various components of leadership. And some editors actually have given this one some thought; it's a fairly decent definition of Transformational Leadership:

Transformational Leadership enhances the motivation, morale, and performance of followers through a variety of mechanisms. These include connecting the follower's sense of identity and self to the project and the collective identity of the organization; being a role model for followers that inspires them and makes them interested; challenging followers to take greater ownership for their work, and understanding the strengths and weaknesses of followers, so the leader can align followers with tasks that enhance their performance.[1]

There are also textbook definitions of Transformational Leadership. In our next chapter, I'm actually going to challenge the notion of leadership being a lateral or a hierarchical metaphor. But James Burns wrote that "leaders and followers make each other advance to a higher level of moral motivation."[2] Elaine Marshall wrote: "It is a process of developing the leadership capacity of an entire team. Transformational Leaders inspire others to achieve what might be considered extraordinary results. Leaders and followers engage with each other, raise each other, and inspire each other."[3]

Randy Dobbs, is a well-known CEO who was with General Electrical during Jack Welch's tenure. In the context of organizational leadership, he

---

1   "Transformational Leadership", Wikipedia.org http://en.wikipedia.org/wiki/Transformational_leadership (accessed March 8 2014).

2   James MacGregor Burns, *Leadership*, 1st ed. (New York: Harper & Row, 1978).

3   Elaine Sorensen Marshall and Elaine S. Marshall, *Transformational Leadership in Nursing: From Expert Clinician to Influential Leader* (New York, NY: Springer, 2011). 3.

gives us five attributes that define Transformational Leadership.[4] These are all based on what we can see in the results. These are the 5 key elements of Transformational Leadership according to Dobbs:

1.) Build a culture

2.) Improve *esprit de corps*

3.) Communicate issues and actions

4.) Change the financial results
(or behavioral/spiritual or other metric)

5.) Leave behind a cadre of future transformational leaders

When I was sixteen or seventeen years old, I was having a tough time in life. It seemed like everybody I knew either moved or died during my sophomore and junior years of high school. There was one guy though who was really helpful to me. He happened to be a staff member at Campus Life Youth for Christ, actually. He was in charge of helping the local teens through the churches engage in various social activities. I went to the burgers bashes, I went to the concerts that were offered to us, and I went to the religious services that were a part of that as well.

During my particular time of need, this minister was there to help me on a personal level, along with other kids in the community. Because he was so helpful to me, long after I graduated from college, I continued to occasionally give him a call on the telephone, just to say hello. I grew up in Chicago, and I had since moved off to the South, where it's much warmer and doesn't snow. He had moved to Northern Michigan, where there was more snow and a little colder temperature. So even though we were now living in different parts of the country, and I was now an adult, I maintained that friendship. I would send him a Christmas card, and I would call him up on the phone and speak to him.

One day, I called him, and he said he had big news.

I said, "What's that?"

He said, "Well, I'm leaving Campus Life Youth for Christ."

I said, "Really? Why?" I was surprised.

He said, "You know, I have four kids. Now they're getting older, and

---

4   Randy Dobbs, *Transformational Leadership: A Blueprint for Real Organizational Change*, 1st ed. (L, Ar: Parkhurst Brothers Inc., Publishers, 2010). 2.

they're going to be going to college. I need to do something that pays the bills. I'm excited. I've taken a new job, and I'm going to be selling hydraulic hose."

I immediately became a little concerned. Was he no longer interested in things of faith or ministering to people or helping people?

He chuckled. "No, I'm still going to be ministering to people, but in a volunteer capacity rather than a paid capacity because like Paul, I'm going to be a tent maker, and earn my living selling hydraulic hoses."

My friend had stayed in youth ministry for many years. It's filled with high stress, high burn out, and low wages. And so I asked him, "You did stay in youth ministry longer than most. What do all the other kids who you've worked with over the years say about this change that you've made? What do they think about it, going from youth ministry to hydraulic hose sales?"

"I'm not really sure," he replied.

And so I said to him, "When you talk on the phone with them, what do you say?"

And he said, "I don't really talk on the phone with them too much."

"But you've been doing youth ministry for almost 20 years; certainly you hear from people."

He said, "Occasionally, after they graduate from high school or if they join the military, they come back and show me the awesome car they bought, or say hello when they're on leave. If they went off to college, they will occasionally call, particularly if they have some difficulties. I get invitations to weddings after they graduate. For the most part, people grow up and move on, and I stop hearing from them."

I said, "Why? You've stayed in the youth ministry for almost 20 years, but you rarely ever hear from anybody, what motivated you to stay in it?"

He said, "Well, you kept calling."

For my friend, leadership was not about helping *most* of the people *most* of the time. For my friend, leadership was about helping *some* of the people *some* of the time, and hoping that those people would then go on to help transform other people. He derived his satisfaction not from becoming the guru of youth ministers and becoming the king of a global empire of related youth ministries, but by hopefully having an impact on some of the kids he worked with over the years, who would then go on to positively impact other people. In my mind, this really is the heart of Transformational Leadership. What Randy Dobbs talks about in his book on Transformation Leadership: Leaving behind a cadre of future Transformational Leaders so that the change is not just about one person, but about the system, the community, and the organization.

I'm going to give you one last definition of Transformational Leadership, a definition that I wrote:

> *Transformational Leadership is a form of synergistic leadership, in which motivation to action comes from the leader's own growth and enthusiasm for new possibilities. Transformational Leadership is a dynamic leadership that recognizes change as a constant and that as a result, leadership is an ongoing function of organizational and individual wellness. Transformational Leadership utilizes processes that has shown efficacy to create lasting change in individuals, communities, organizations, and even in the world.*

In the next chapter, I'm going to answer the question: Is Transformational Leadership really more effective than other forms of leaderships? And I'm going to touch on some of the other forms of leaderships that academics like Bernard Bass have written about and that are studied in academic circles. Our goal in this book is to give you a foundation for making true change in your world, in your communities, and within yourself as well.

Chapter Two:
Transformational Leadership Explained

In this chapter, I'm going to explain how Transformational Leadership is different from other forms of leadership, and I'm also going to answer an important question:

How do we know that Transformational Leadership
is an effective approach?

Fortunately, there are many academic programs which study leadership. At Bakke Graduate University, for example, Transformational Leadership is studied at the intersection of theology, business, and ministry. In educational leadership programs, Transformational Leadership is studied as a way of creating change within educational organizations and educational systems. Transformational leadership has been studied in healthcare settings, in military settings, corporate and sales settings, and in a number of other contexts. We have the results from these studies, and these studies tell us that Transformational Leadership as contrasted with other forms of leadership yields excellent results.

One study, focusing on Transformational Leadership in an academic setting of 89 schools in Singapore, found that Transformational Leadership had significant add-on effects to transactional leadership in the prediction of organizational commitment, organizational citizenship, and teacher satisfaction.[5]

---

5   William Koh, Richard Steers, and James Terborg, "The Effects of Transformational Leadership on Teacher Attitudes and Student Performance in Singapore," *Journal of Organizational Behavior* 16, no. 4 (1995).

Transformational leadership has been studied in healthcare settings – nursing, counseling, and other settings. Transformational leadership outcomes were measured among clinical staff in a hospital setting, and it was found that Transformational Leadership is significantly related to increased satisfaction, increased staff well-being, decreased burn out, and decreased overall stress in staff.[6]

Sometimes, since I'm a counselor, people ask me about Transformational Leadership in the counseling setting or the mental health setting. In a 2006 study, 303 public sector mental health professionals were surveyed about supervisors' leadership styles while new evidence-based protocols in service delivery were adopted, essentially during managed care. The study found that both transformational and transactional leadership were positively associated with providers having more positive attitudes towards the adoption of evidence-based practice.[7]

My son is in the military. He's an 11B – that's infantry, active duty. So I'm interested of course in leadership training in the military because he has gone through a variety of different leadership courses. In an experiment to put Transformational Leadership to the test, 54 military leaders were trained in Transformational Leadership or were part of a control group using eclectic leadership strategies. The results indicated more leaders in the experimental group, this would be the Transformational Leadership group, had more positive impact on direct followers' development and on indirect followers' performance than the leaders in the control group (those who went through eclectic leadership training).[8]

Sometimes, I'm asked, "Does Transformational Leadership translate across cultures? Is it an approach to leadership that can be used cross-culturally?" Well, studies confirm that Transformational Leadership does work well in various cultures. In almost every area where the efficacy of Transformational Leadership has been studied from a results-oriented perspective, Transformational Leadership is shown to be an empirically-validated form of leadership. In fact, even church leadership journals favor Transformational Leadership in community-based and non-profit sectors. Journals in healthcare man-

---

6   D. Weberg, "Transformational Leadership and Staff Retention: An Evidence Review with Implications for Healthcare Systems," *Nurs Adm Q* 34, no. 3 (2010).

7   G. A. Aarons, "Transformational and Transactional Leadership: Association with Attitudes toward Evidence-Based Practice," *Psychiatr Serv* 57, no. 8 (2006).

8   Taly Dvir et al., "Impact of Transformational Leadership on Follower Development and Performance: A Field Experiment," *Academy of Management journal* 45, no. 4 (2002).

agement, manufacturing, and distribution sectors prefer Transformational Leadership.

Now, why is this empirical research important? It's important not because it means that Transformational Leadership is the only viable strategy—there are other approaches to leadership and some of them have efficacy in some situations—but the reason why we want to study empirical research as it relates to Transformational Leadership is it confirms that Transformational Leadership is a proven strategy. Research shows that in new situations with new leaders and new communities, you are more likely at the outset to experience desired results when you use an approach founded on Transformational Leadership.

As a therapist in clinical settings, I prefer treatment strategies that are based on research. An example of this might be a new client who comes to me for the treatment of social phobia. There are a lot of different ways to treat social phobia, and over the years we've improved on the treatment of social phobia and anxiety disorder by adding to our body of knowledge and changing the techniques that are employed to help people experience change. However, some of the methods that have been used in the past are outdated, and other methods demonstrate less acceptable results in broad clinical studies than other methods. One example of a therapeutic approach that's been abandoned for the most part is the cathartic psychodynamic approaches. If you're not a therapist, you can think Sigmund Freud here. Sigmund Freud was really the architect of this psychodynamic approach or the personality restructuring approach. And in the current area of research, an approach based on contextual psychology is considered an outcome-based treatment; most therapists have abandoned the theories and the methods of Sigmund Freud and the earliest approaches. This means that, while I can't say I would *never* utilize a psychodynamic approach with anyone, I would favor an evidence-based approach with most new clients–something that we often call "contextual psychology."[9]

We need to recognize that people are different. Leaders are different. Therapists are different. Managers are different. Situations are different. The way I see it in therapy is this: Suppose I'm meeting a new client with social anxiety. I've never met this person before, and I don't know much about them. But because the client expects results or relief in the first session (at least at

---

9   Richard Nongard, *Contextual Psychology: Integrating Mindfulness-Based Approaches into Effective Therapy* (Scottsdale, AZ: Peachtree Professional Education, Inc., 2014).

some level), I'm going to utilize a method of contextual psychology, one called "ACT Therapy," as my first choice. This maximizes the potential for success in providing a solution. I can more efficiently impact more people by choosing an evidence-based protocol rather than simply drawing from my prior experiences or using that which is most familiar to me.

At a later point in working with a client, I might re-evaluate the treatment plan. And for a rare client, I might move towards the converse of what I usually do and choose a psychodynamic approach or even a different approach that is not used very often. Medical doctors, of course, do the exact same thing. The first medication prescribed is the one with which most patients find success. The doctor does this to maximize the potential for success as early as possible in treating medical problems. But this does not mean that with some patients at some time, a different medication is prescribed, or that a change in medication to one less commonly used, or even one that's sometimes regarded as less than effective is used. In almost every profession from business management to sales to marketing to organizational outcomes, evidence-based strategies are considered to be best practices; therefore, they are generally preferred or favored as a first approach.

Evidence-based leadership means that we will favor the vast empirical data surrounding the efficacy of Transformational Leadership. It is our first choice because it maximizes the likelihood of successes and outcomes that are desired. At times though, we might, in unique situations, adopt and incorporate transactional leadership into our Transformational Leadership or our charismatic leadership. Or perhaps in some situations, we might abandon Transformational Leadership all together to adopt a unique or less common leadership style or leadership strategy.

Before we go further and study some of the various models of Transformational Leadership, I want us to abandon a hierarchical understanding of Transformational Leadership. Again, the reason why is simple, most of us reading this book, are not going to become the president of a small nation, we're probably not going to become the chief executive officer of an international corporation. Leadership is often viewed as something for top executives to study or a topic only of interest to people in positions of power. One of the things that is really unique about Transformational Leadership is that, in Transformational Leadership, we can abandon the idea of a hierarchy.

On the second page of the first chapter of the book, *Transformational Leadership*, Bernard Bass and Ronald Riggio write: "Leadership is not just the province of people at the top. Leadership could occur at all levels and by any individual." Bass and Riggio go on to advocate the process of leaders training leaders who are below them, retaining the metaphor of a hierarchy. But I want to challenge the idea that in leadership there is a top or a bottom. I actually think height is a poor metaphor, and the students of Transformational Leadership see it as the core of connecting in a meaningful and valuable way to others rather than just to wait to accomplish the pyramid effect of task completion.

My friend who is who is the hotel clerk whom we discussed in Chapter 1 is not trying to get to the top. She is, however, trying to connect to people in a meaningful way, and connect those people to each other in a meaningful way, which will transform the community where she works.

The first step in dismantling the hierarchy is really to change the language we associate with leadership. For example, leaders are responsible to train those they work with and must be open to being trained by those with whom they work. Author of the book *Scaling Up Excellence*, Stanford professor Bob Sutton argues that hierarchy is not a bad thing—in fact, it's both inevitable and needed.[10] But Sutton is speaking in the context of organizational management, and while I agree that hierarchy as an organizational concept is both inevitable and needed, leadership transcends hierarchy. It really is much more personal, which is why everybody can be a transformational leader. Even within the hierarchy or organizational structure, leadership can be present or conceptualized as a matrix with hierarchical, lateral, and even bottom-up incarnations.

I ended Chapter One with some definitions of Transformational Leadership. In this chapter, I want to build on those definitions and talk about some models of Transformational Leadership.

Bass and Riggio offer a model which is widely used in academia. Transformational leadership is contrasted with transactional leadership by Bass and Riggio. The simple definition of transactional leadership, which was originally offered by Burns in 1978, is that transactional leaders are those who lead through social exchange. It's important to note that Bass and Riggio based much of their work in articulating Transformational Leadership on the original work of Burns and his description of a new kind of leadership in 1978. Burns presents as an example of transactional leadership the politician who offers something valuable to different constituent groups in exchange for

---

10   Robert Sutton, "Hierarchy Is Good. Hierarchy Is Essential. And Less Isn't Always Better" http://blogs.parc.com/blog/2014/02/hierarchy-is-good-hierarchy-is-essential-and-less-isnt-always-better/ (accessed March 8, 2014).

votes. The politician, for example, gains power to lead by voting for legislation that is favored by constituent groups, who then in turn offer political support to that candidate through their votes. Hence, there is a transaction between the leader and the followers, between the politician and the voters.

As a therapist who in the distant past worked in adolescent psychiatric settings and also in criminal justice mental health settings that were based on behaviorism and level system, I have seen the tasks of therapy implemented in a transactional model. In this model, a patient might get certain rewards for certain behaviors. And this is an approach to therapy I found both ineffective and limiting in those early experiences. I've even seen ministers create systems based on transactional leadership. And certainly in the world of business, it is often present. It sounds kind of like this: "I will tell you what you need to know and do, and you will then get a paycheck." This is a classic example of transactional leadership. Most of us use a form of transactional leadership almost everyday—or actually of transactional influence. In sales, loyalty cards are an example of transactional leadership or transactional influence rather than the other forms of influence and leadership. And in the end, loyalty cards can actually cost a business when the loyalty program has changed and the transactions stop or are modified.

Transformational leaders then, according to Bass and Riggio, as contrasted with transactional leaders, "help followers grow in developing into leaders by responding to individual follower's needs by empowering them and by aligning the objectives and goals of the individual followers, the leader, the group, and the larger organization."[11] Really, in Bass and Riggio's model of Transformational Leadership, alignment is the key concept. Another term for this could be "parallel programming."

Well, how is Transformational Leadership implemented if it's not done in a transactional way, if it's not done to an exchange? According to Bass and Riggio, "transformational leaders empower followers and pay attention to their individual needs and personal development, helping followers develop their own leadership potential."[12] This is conceptualized through four main components of Transformational Leadership.

---

11   Bernard M. Bass and Ronald E. Riggio, *Transformational Leadership*, 2nd ed. (Mahwah, N.J.: L. Erlbaum Associates, 2006). 3.

12   Ibid. 4.

The Four Components of Transformational Leadership

Bass and Riggio identify four main components to Transformational Leadership, which we will discuss in turn:

- Idealized Influence
- Inspirational Motivation
- Intellectual Stimulation
- Individualized Consideration

Idealized Influence:

When I was 18, I got what was really one of my first jobs. I was a waiter at a Mexican restaurant called Chi-Chi's. Chi-Chi's Mexican Restaurant actually used to be all over the country. I haven't seen any for years so I think the whole chain is out of business. I had a boss and his name was Chuck. Chuck actually started years before as a dish man working in the kitchen. He worked his way up to line cook and then became a dinner cook. He held other jobs in the restaurant including bartender and waiter at various times. He had worked his way up through management to become a general manager of the Chi-Chi's store. Because this was one of my first jobs, I did not know what to expect in a general manager—and I've longed to have a general manager like Chuck ever since. In that year or two where I was a waiter at Chi-Chi's Mexican Restaurant in college, Chuck, as the general manager, could be found in his office doing paper work, or at the front line helping the cooks stay out of the weeds, or in the bathroom fixing a plumbing problem, or helping waiters carry out their food. Chuck exemplified idealized influence. This refers to the ability to influence others through example or modeling.

In Neuro-Linguistic Programming, an entire discipline devoted to personal change and empowerment, the idea of transformation is predicated on modeling. Richard Bandler and John Grinder the co-creators of NLP began by studying those who were effective. They began by studying three particularly effective therapists in the early days: Fritz Perls, Virginia Satir, and Milton Erickson. They created a concept for change based on modeling. This is something that Tony Robbins has done in his coaching and empowerment courses: helping people to find exemplars and models from which they can learn. The core idea of idealized influence is that of an exemplar, where a person leads through example.

In Alcoholics Anonymous and other Twelve-Step programs, pure leadership occurs through a sponsor. And a well-known admonition within these Twelve-Step groups to help a person find a sponsor is to pick somebody "who has what you want." For many people, this aspect of Transformational Leadership is one of the most difficult, and the reason is simple: none of us is perfect—in fact, most of us are far from perfect. Inside our heads are thoughts, ideas, and desires that we really don't want anyone to know about, especially the people who are close to us. It's this fear of transparency or inadequacy that often keeps up from realizing our full potential. It is for this reason that later chapters of this book will specifically address this aspect of your leadership development. You're going to learn that to be a transformational leader, you must embrace your humility rather than create the facade of power in order to manifest idealized influence. I'm going to teach you some of the tasks that will empower you to be a genuine leader, and I'm going to guide you through some specific strategies for doing so.

Inspirational Motivation:

The second component of Transformational Leadership is inspirational motivation. In inspirational motivation, the idea is to motivate others. But to do this, there must a vision that people want to move towards. The transformational leader articulates this vision, whether it's to one person or whether it's to a group. But really, this is more than just sharing what we think something should be like. It's helping people to adopt a vision as their own vision, something that they can embrace.

In order to inspire, a leader must be genuine–this is a theme that you're going to hear throughout this book. Inspirational motivation helps people to genuinely embrace and adopt new ideas. Although there are many methods for doing this, two strategies have been particularly useful to me: first, communicating a vision congruent with the primary representational system of other people; and second, helping people to adopt this vision as their own idea, creating ownership of a new future.

I'd like to expand on how to communicate a vision congruent with the primary representational system of others. In the Appendix A, you'll find a one-page assessment tool called, *The Nongard Assessment of Primary Representational Systems*. This is a questionnaire that I've developed for the clients with whom I have worked. When I have a new client I've never met the before, this is one of the forms I give them. It takes them about a minute or two to fill out. The applications go far beyond the therapy office.

The questionnaire consists of ten questions, and it asks the individual to make one of three choices about how they would respond to the situation. What I want them to do is pick the one that they would do first, or most, or most likely in the given situation. There are ten questions; only one answer per question. Every now and then, people say, "But there are a couple of things I would do." It's okay if you would a couple of things. I ask, "Which one would be your first inclination or which one appeals to you most powerfully?"

Then, there a score key provided. It's in the appendix, and you add up all the A's, you add up all the B's, and you add up all the C's. This helps us identify the primary learning/communication style of the respondent: auditory, visual, or kinesthetic.

What I'd like you to do right now is actually pause, take *The Nongard Assessment of Primary Representational Systems* and add up your scores at the bottom, determining whether or not you're primarily a visual person, an auditory person, or kinesthetic person.

Now that you've read and completed the assessment of your primary representational systems, you have some scores. You have scores under A (which is visual), B (which is auditory), or C (which is kinesthetic). One of those numbers is highest. This would be your dominant area. There's not a right or wrong answer. People are different. As a leader who's trying to communicate with either a group of individuals or an individual with whom I'm working, I'm going to have an easier time building rapport and connecting with that person when I can communicate my vision in a way that is congruent with their communication style or their communication strategy.

So, if I'm working with somebody who is visual, I am probably going to use visual language in my communication. For example, "See the bigger picture. As you look out over the horizon of your future..." Those are examples of language patterns which are based on a visual connection with a visual learner. If I had somebody who's an auditory learner, I'm probably going to communicate a vision congruent with their primary representational system by using auditory language. For example, "As you make these changes, it's almost as if you can hear that internal voice guiding you and directing you in the decisions that you make." That is an example of an auditory communication strategy. The kinesthetic person is a person who's very tactile. They learn by touching, by being absorbed into things. So, I might communicate using kinesthetic language, that is, very tactile-oriented language, to communicate my vision. I might say, "And as we make changes, you will feel a sense of lightness as the burden of the workload is shared among many different individuals." That is an example of a way of communicating a vision using language that's consistent with the results in this questionnaire.

In a later chapter, I'm going to come back and re-visit this idea and add some more depth to it. But I thought it was important right at the beginning of this book that you recognize what your own learning style is. When I was working with people in couples counseling, I found my knowledge of primary representational systems very helpful. I had worked with a lot of couples who come in fighting. They're arguing; they're going back and forth. But as the outside observer, I'm sitting across the room from them; as I listen to them talk and argue with each other, sometimes with great passion, I'm amazed at how many times I recognize they're actually in agreement. They're actually saying the same thing.

Where is the conflict coming from? They're not understanding each other because they're not communication their ideas in a way that is congruent with the primary representational system of the other. So, the wife is using kinesthetic language, saying to the husband, "The problems that we are experiencing are a weight on my shoulders. I feel a sense of depression that's just dragging me down." In his communication, he's using visual language. He's saying something like, "Whenever I look out at the future of our relationship, what I don't see is…" And I recognized that as I listen to these arguments, their issue is not that they can't come to an agreement, but that they're not able to make a connection because they don't understand each other's primary representational systems. In fact, to be leader in the family, one must understand the primary representational system of the children, of the other spouse, and any extended family members who have close relationships with those within that nuclear family.

Intellectual Stimulation:

The third component of Transformational Leadership is intellectual stimulation. Transformational leaders encourage creativity, questioning, and solutions from within the organization without regard to status or position. Transformational leaders recognize that the front line employee might have the creative insight to problem solve in a way that actually has global implications for a large company, and that recognition fosters an environment in which intellectual growth, learning, and creativity are valued such that they become the standard. To use an old cliché, Transformational Leadership is not about giving people fish, but about teaching them how to fish. It is in many cases a training process of developing others through intellectual stimulation and intellectual intelligence, as well as social intelligence (a term that we're going to define in one of our later chapters).

Individualized Consideration:

The fourth component of Transformational Leadership is called "individualized consideration." Leaders that have a lasting impact are mentors who, according to Randy Dobbs, "leave behind a cadre of leaders."[13] This is really the transformation in Transformational Leadership. First, we transform ourselves into effective leaders. Second, we transform others. And third, we create a perpetual motion machine of leadership, in which one person goes on to impact another person. Just like Bob in my example in Chapter One, who influenced me. And I have hopefully through my work as a professor influenced others.

Transformational Leadership provides a great deal of satisfaction for leaders who are therapists, pastors, coaches, teachers, mentors, nurses, health-care professionals, supervisors, and executives. It means that the value of working with one person is not less important than the experience of working with many people. When our work is done right, each person we work with impacts others. It creates a pyramid of transformation. In many cases, this occurs on an intergenerational level.

I was blessed last summer to have the opportunity to work for a short period of time with a group in Phoenix, Arizona, called *Neighborhood Ministries*. This group has been on the forefront of Christian community development for over 33 years. In 33 years of impacting the community, they have influenced families on a multi-generational basis. The summer that I was there working with them, I got the chance to see children of volunteers who became volunteers because they were affected when they were children in the program. I saw parents and grandparents who had actually participated in the transformation and renewal within that community. The goal of *Neighborhood Ministries* is to be the home of the next generation of Arizona leaders. They encourage education, family participation, spiritual maturity, and financial

---

13   Dobbs.

success within the community. And all of these things are done through a plan that affects a large number of people at one time but through one-on-one relationships, which then become the source of this perpetual motion machine, transforming a community, a neighborhood, a city, and a state.

Important Points Summarized

At this point, I've discussed several key points in Chapters One and Two about Transformational Leadership.

First, there's a need for leadership in both large and small organizations, and even in one-on-one interpersonal settings.

Two, Transformational Leadership is necessary not to find the most effective route to change, but because everything is always changing.

Three, Transformational Leadership enhances the motivation, morale and performance of followers through a variety of mechanisms, and these can be learned.

Four, Transformational Leadership is a synergistic leadership, where motivation to action comes from the leader's own growth and enthusiasm for new possibilities.

Five, Transformational Leadership is empirically-based and considered an evidence-based practice.

Six, one popular model of Transformational Leadership—Bass and Riggio—identify four key components: idealized influence, inspirational motivation, intellectual stimulation, and individualized consideration.

Seven, Transformational Leadership transcends organizational models. It can be employed hierarchically, laterally, from the bottom-up, from left to right, or from right to left. It can even exist apart from any organization.

The Competencies Required of a Transformational Leader

As we move into the next couple of chapters, I want to recognize that you participated in this book not to simply learn about leadership, but to undoubtedly become a more effective leader. And so, what competencies must you develop to accomplish this goal? Well, there are five competencies which have been identified based on the four key components of Transformational Leadership; throughout the rest of this book, one of the things that I'm going to try to do is to really teach you some strategies that can help you to accomplish mastering these competencies.

The five competencies are as follows:

- Action Learning
- Envisioning
- Communicating a Vision
- Managing Impressions
- Empowering Followers

The first, identified by Conger and Benjamin,[14] is a strategy of action learning. This is called "critical evaluation and problem detection." Action learning is a process in which people learn in teams, bringing together processing experiences and creating new perceptual positions, fostering new beliefs, and expanding the repertoire of interventions. A formula in action learning can be presented this way:

$$L = P + Q + R$$

Learning is equal to Programming plus Questioning plus Reflection; and might I add, learning is predicated on the power of the group.

The second competency is envisioning. This is all about creative thinking—not only learning but also unlearning experiences. As a therapist, I spend as much time helping clients unlearn things as often as I do helping them people learn new things.

A third competency in Transformational Leadership is communication skills for conveying a vision. I've already shared with you a powerful tool—the Primary Representational System—which we'll revisit. This is an excellent starting point that works along with tools for assertive communication, whether that's in management, therapy, or even interpersonal relationships.

The fourth competency of Transformational Leadership is impression management: being an effective model in communication–both verbal and non-verbal, including our body language, appearance, social skills.

---

14   Jay Alden Conger and Beth Benjamin, *Building Leaders: How Successful Companies Develop the Next Generation*, 1st ed., The Jossey-Bass Business & Management Series (San Francisco: Jossey-Bass, 1999).

And the fifth competency is knowing both how and when to empower followers. Good skills for empowering others include helping people to adopt change as their own, decision-making, and cutting through red tape.

When we talk about these five competencies, several questions arise: Are they really effective? Can these competencies be learned? Yes, they can. The empirical data tells us this.

Bass and Riggio, in their textbook on Transformational Leadership, share outcome studies in each of these areas that indicate that Transformational Leadership training is highly effective. Their studies address shop supervisors, community leaders, and bank managers. And beyond Riggio and Bass's textbook, many different applications of Transformational Leadership, competencies, have been utilized by a number of different organizations: large and small, profit and non-profit, faith-based and secular-based, governmental and non-governmental. And all of these studies share one common truth. That truth is that Transformational Leadership is a highly effective approach to leadership and that these competencies can be taught to others.

Chapter Three:

Developing Your Personal Leadership

In this chapter, we're going to be moving from learning about Transformational Leadership to a more personal focus on our own development as a leader. We know from the previous chapter that leadership can be taught. The previous chapter included an empirical basis for such a conclusion. But most people come to leadership as they are–not yet formally trained, but endowed with certain desires or personality characteristics that seem to exude leadership. What characteristics do you have that make you a good leader? The starting point for any endeavor, and certainly leadership, really is the strengths that you already possess. This is going to be your foundation for your ability to transform both yourself and others.

Whenever I'm speaking before a group, I always like to ask if anyone in the room is trustworthy, loyal, helpful, friendly, courteous, kind, obedient, cheerful, thrifty, brave, clean, or reverent. Whenever I ask that of a group, people in the group do two things. Usually, they'll begin to recognize that some of those actually apply to them; and second, they usually have a smile on their face because these twelve characteristics come from the Boys Scout Law, which is often our very first introduction to defining leadership competencies.

Any discussion of leadership training then must ask the question: "Does success in leadership hinge on personality traits?" This is really important because in the field of psychology, personality traits are often viewed as inflexible or predetermined. Our diagnosis of personality disorder has historically been understood as a lifelong constant. And the converse of that, personality strengths, are often perceived something that is either innate or learned early on. But studies do find that there are significant relationships between leadership perceptions and certain psychological or social traits.

The Five Factor Model gives us various dimensions of traits which have a statistical correlation to leadership. Sofia Sjoberg at Stockholm University writes, "Support for the Five Factor Model as an organizing framework for personality when looking at leadership has shown to be relevant; therefore, this is the model most common in empirical research."[15] This does not, however, mean that the Big Five Traits are the only form of analysis which is appropriate to predicting our leadership criteria.

The Five Factor Model

These are the five factors:

- Openness
- Conscientiousness
- Extroversion
- Agreeableness
- Neuroticism

Openness:

Openness refers to the curious nature of a person, their inquisitive approach to the world, their ability to generate ideas, multiple experiences, and characteristics related to industriousness.

Conscientiousness:

This is the ability to be self-regulating, have impulse control, and maintain attention on the present. This is a popular topic in corporate training right now, the idea of Mindfulness.

Extroversion:

This encompasses characteristics of communication like assertiveness and energy, positive emotions, and the ability to both stimulate others and derive stimulation or energy from others.

---

15   Sofia Sjöberg, "What Do We Know About Traits Predicting Leader Emergence and Leader Effectiveness?," in *Frontiers in Leadership Research*, Department of Learning, Informatics, Management & Ethics (Karolinska Institutet).

Agreeableness:

This really deals with the idea of cooperation or collaboration, and trust vs. suspicion. Have you ever had a business experience where you've gone in to create a transaction with somebody else but their suspicious nature kept you from feeling that rapport had been developed, and maybe even kept you from entering into that relationship?

Neuroticism:

As a therapist, I'm accustomed to using the word neuroticism. When I use that for a non-therapeutic audience, often they think: "Oh, that means a person is crazy, correct?" And that's really not what we're referring to here in the Five Factor Model. We're talking about a person who easily experiences negative states; a person who is irritable, restless, discontent as their normal state of being. And these are characteristics which have a correlation to difficulty in leading others. Remember that it is a factor in predicting leadership ability, not a trait necessary for leadership.

Later on in this chapter, you're going to really examine the strengths that you currently possess, and I'm going to have you use a couple of different approaches to bring to the table your own personality characteristics to help you develop your leadership potential. The Big Five are a starting point for us, but they're not the only predictors of leadership.

In reviewing these items, begin asking yourself: "Which of these traits do I already possess and how can I begin to apply them in my interpersonal relationships with others?" I have a theory that leadership is something we are, rather than something we do. We don't *do* leadership. We *are* leaders. As a result, leadership qualities are present not only when we do organizational management or professional mentoring; they are also to present in all of our interpersonal interactions, from dealing with the family dog to a stranger we meet on the subway.

How else can we assess the characteristics of Transformational Leadership? Any academic study of Transformational Leadership needs to incorporate, or at least help you become aware of, various tools which measure leadership characteristics and qualities. Bernard Bass and Bruce Aviolo have developed an assessment tool designed for organizational settings called the *Multi-Factor Leadership Questionnaire*. It's available from www.mindgarden.com. This is really a standard assessment tool in understanding Transformational Leadership. The current version is referred to as the MLQ 5X or the

Standard MLQ. As you read journals about Transformational Leadership and measures in academic settings, the MLQ is something with which you're going to become very familiar.

The MLQ measures, explains and demonstrates to individuals the key factors that set truly exceptional leaders apart from the marginal ones. The MindGarden.com website tells us that the MLQ distinguishes between effective and ineffective leaders at all organizational levels. It assesses the effectiveness of an entire organization's leadership, and it's been validated across cultures and across different types of organizations. One of the things that I like about the MLQ is that it's relatively easy to administer. It requires about 15 minutes or less for somebody to complete. And it has been extensively researched and validated, as a quick search on scholar.google.com will demonstrate.

The MLQ provides an excellent relationship between survey data and organizational outcome. And that's really important because one of the questions we have is: "Does Transformational Leadership make a difference?" And the MLQ has really been adopted as the benchmark measure for Transformational Leadership.

Now, it is true that there have been criticisms of the MLQ, just like there are of any tool that purports to measure anything. But the MLQ, because it has been standardized in academic settings, has undergone a number of different revisions, hence the current version being the MLQ 5X.

It's composed of skill assessments that examine a full range of leadership behaviors. The classic form includes both self and rater forms. In other words, you can use this to self-score, or this form could be used by, for example, employees to rate a supervisor or a manager. The range of leadership behaviors that it measures include the four components or characteristics of Transformational Leadership that I've previously discussed: idealized attributes/ idealized behaviors, inspirational motivation, intellectual stimulation and individualized consideration.

The second focus of its questions is transactional leadership, measuring contingent reward and management by exception from an active perspective. It also measures passive and avoidant leadership traits, which might be management by exception in a passive mode and a laissez-faire approach to leadership. And then it measures what the outcome of this leadership is. Is there extra effort? Is it effective? Are those who are engaged with the leader satisfied with leadership?

The way the MLQ is set up is that 45 descriptive statements are rated on a Likert Scale. A Likert Scale is a scale that could be 1 to 10 or 1 to 5—in the case of the MLQ, it's actually 0 to 4—but each number represents a measure of an equal interval. So for example, on the MLQ, 0 represents "not at all"; 1 represents "once in a while"; 2 represents "sometimes"; 3 represents "fairly often"; and 4 represents "frequently, if not always."

Here are some examples of questions that are on the MLQ offered by Mind Garden:

Example: This questionnaire describes the leadership style of the above-mentioned individual as you perceive it. Please answer all items on this answer sheet. If an item is irrelevant, or if you are unsure or do not know the answer, leave the answer blank. Please answer this questionnaire anonymously.[16]

Forty-five descriptive statements are listed on the following pages. Judge how frequently each statement fits the person you are describing. Use the following rating scale:

0	1	2	3	4
Not At All	Once in a While	Sometimes	Fairly Often	Frequently, if not always

1.	Talks optimistically about the future	0	1	2	3	4
2.	Spends time teaching and coaching	0	1	2	3	4
3.	Avoids making decisions	0	1	2	3	4

At the conclusion of all 45 questions, some numerical scores are produced and this helps us to identify Transformational Leadership, transactional leadership, passive/avoidant traits, and the outcomes of leadership.

Here is a question: If you're getting ready to do a dissertation or you want to study your own effectiveness so that you can become more self-aware, or if you'd like to study in a corporate setting the perception of employees of a manager or supervisor, can a tool like the MLQ really be useful in understanding leadership? Again, it's been empirically validated to yield best practices in almost all professions and interactions. The MindGarden.com webpage states: "The MLQ identifies the characteristics of a transformational leader and helps individuals discover how they measure up in their own eyes and in the eyes of those with whom they work."[17]

There are other assessment tools out there, but what separates the MLQ from other assessments of leadership is its wide use of academic research in organizational settings. Paul Kirkbride identifies it as the most widely used assessment tool to Transformational Leadership.[18] The MLQ has been cited as a reliable tool in many different publications. The MLQ in light of the revisions that have been made over the years is considered by most to be both a reliable and valid tool: "Regardless of the theoretical or measurement shortcomings, our results indicate that the current version of the MLQ, Form 5x, is a valid and reliable instrument that can adequately measure the nine components comprising the full range theory of leadership."[19] Although the MLQ form 5X—and indeed any leadership survey instrument—will never account for all possible leadership dimensions, it represents a foundation from which to conduct further research and to expand our understandings of the new models of leadership.

Personalizing your own Leadership Attributes

To this point, we've reviewed assessment of leadership from an academic perspective using the Big Five Factors and the MLQ. My hope is that even though I've presented this as an academic exercise, you've actually internalized these ideas and have begun to think about how they manifest in your life. From this point forward, each of our chapters will become more and more personal–focused on you and your journey as a leader. Notice that we are talking about your present journey. I did not say, "When you *become* a leader…" I said: "*As* a leader." Throughout the rest of the book, I'm going to focus on key applications of leadership in your life. You will have the opportunity to use it beginning at this moment, today.

Throughout my career as a therapist, I've been empowered by approaches to psychology that have been contrary to the traditional model of

---

17   Bernard M. Bass and Bruce Avolio, "The Benchmark Measure for Transformational Leadership" http://www.mindgarden.com/products/mlq.htm#overview (accessed March 8, 2014).

18   Paul Kirkbride, "Developing Transformational Leaders: The Full Range Leadership Model in Action," *Industrial and Commercial Training* 38, no. 1 (2006).

19   John Antonakis, Bruce Avolio, and Nagaraj Sivasibramaniam, "Context and Leadership: An Examination of the Nine-Factor Full-Range Leadership Theory Using the Multifactor Leadership Questionnaire," *The Leadership Quarterly* 14, (2003).

understanding human experience. The traditional model is the pathological or a diagnostically-oriented approach. I've been an advocate of alternatives to the diagnostic and statistical manual, such as Donald Clifton's Strength Psychology and the approaches of Positive Psychology as articulated in the writings of Martin Seligman. As a business executive and corporate consultant, I have employed a model that applies Positive Psychology in the context of either community organizational development or the approach of appreciative inquiry.

In both business and psychotherapy, there's a natural tendency to evaluate either a client, a community, or a corporation that is making change through a lens of problem-identification and problem-resolution. In this approach, the predominant approach to change in almost every setting is to diagnose a problem, to assess deficits, and to try to fix what is broken. Not only is this the most expensive approach is terms of dollars and resources, but it's actually the most difficult approach. The approach of positive psychology and the approach of appreciative inquiry are to some extent contrarian in that not only do they function in the matter that's 180 degrees opposite to the deficit-based model: They actually ignore problems; they ignore deficits; they ignore pathology; they ignore diagnosis. For many, this is such a foreign idea that utilizing such an approach is considered a drastic measure. Therapists have a hard time fathoming working with clients without a diagnosis. When I suggest it to them, I get questions like: "But how are we going to get paid?" This is because to a large extent, the reimbursement system is based on a pathological model of diagnosis and treatment. In business, whenever such ideas are introduced, the executives sometimes shout out, "But how are we going to fix what's broken in the system if we aren't assessing what is wrong?"

On a practical level, when a company's on the precipice of a major change like a merger or a cyclical recession, executives often balk at an approach that is based on appreciative inquiry, saying, "We can't afford to look at what's right until we cut out the cost of doing what's wrong." But this is interesting—the deficit model is not what the research backs. Research is on the side of the strengths-based model. Tom Rath writes, "In stark contrast [to common expectations], our studies indicate that people who do have the opportunity to focus on their strengths are six times more likely to be engaged in their jobs and more than three times as likely to report having an excellent quality of life in general."[20]

---

20   Tom Rath, *Strenghts Finder 2.0* (New York, NY: Gallup Press, 2007).

There are really two ways to run a staff meeting. We could bring everyone in, have them sit in a round circle, have them all identify a problem which is frustrating to them, and then try to brainstorm solutions to those problems. But all of the energy of that group will be focused on what's wrong and never pay attention to what's right. The opposite is, to have anybody who is having turmoil and strife and difficulty during a period of change come in and instead of talking about what's wrong, each person identifies one thing that's right in the company today, one thing that's right with their fellow employees today. The approach of Tom Rath is actually the approach of the late Donald Clifton–he's been considered the grandfather of positive psychology, and his own company was purchased by Gallup. Over the last 40 years, this company had studied 34 themes and ideas for action. All of these are based on identifying strengths. Rath's best-selling book, *Strengths Finder 2.0* describes each of those 34 attributes that have been studied for the past 40 years.

Today is your starting point in mastering a new approach to leadership, and that is to begin with understanding your own strengths. Instead of having you look at the beginning of this book saying, "What's keeping me from being a great leader or holding me back from being a great leader?" I'm going to make the assumption that you are already a leader. Leadership is not about becoming something as much as it is utilizing something. In life, we have both strengths and resources. And by taking an inventory of your strengths, you are already leading. By drawing from your strengths rather than trying to fix what's wrong so you can become a leader, you end the never ending problem of not being ready for a leadership role. You transcend the moment to being a leader right now, right here as you read these pages.

I really want to encourage you to utilize the resources from the Gallup Strengths Center, those created by Tom Rath and Donald Clifton. In addition to *Strengths Finder 2.0,* Gallup Press has published another great book called *Strengths-based Leadership.* These are actually tools that you can use to identify your strengths so that you can maximize your potential right now. In addition to that, there are many others tools that can be useful in helping you to identify your strengths and your resources. Years ago I developed a tool called the *Nongard Strength and Resources Inventory.* The *Nongard Strength and Resources Inventory* is something that I have provided for you in an appendix. Although I use it in therapy, I think that you'll probably find applications for the NSRI in a variety of different settings, ranging from community development to corporate training. The NSRI is conveniently presented on one page and is divided into six sections as follows.

The first section measures the practical and useful things that a person possesses. The second section measures the interaction with self and others. The third block of the *Nongard Strength and Resources Inventory* measures education and job skills. The fourth block measures personal attributes and abilities. The fifth measures personal interest and abilities. And the sixth measures social and situational supports. What I'd like you to do in a moment is actually go to the appendix that contains the blank form for the NSRI, and I'd like you to actually follow the instructions and go through each of these areas, identifying your strengths and your resources.

But before you do that, let me make a distinction between strengths and resources. Strengths really are those internal characteristics that we have that help us to problem solve. For example, strengths include being trustworthy, loyal, helpful, friendly, kind, obedient, cheerful, thrifty, brave, clean, and reverent—again, from the Boys Scout Law. In fact, the Personal Attributes and Abilities section actually addresses traits that have been identified as being 24 core character strengths.

The NSRI is a quick five-minute assessment of an individual's perception of not only their strengths, but also the resources they possess (see appendix B). Resources are a bit different than strengths. The resources are the practical things available to you to help you solve any problem. So for example if I lost my job, if I became unemployed, what resources do I have? Well, I have a phone. People can call me, and I can do an interview. I have a car, so I can get there. I have a backup car. I actually own four cars because I have two teenagers and my wife has her own car, so there's always a car to get to work if I have to. What other resources do I have? Well, I have references. So resources are different from strengths. Strengths are those internal attributes and characteristics. Resources are, in any given situation, the external things available to me to problem solve. The NSRI is one tool that you can feel free to adapt to your individual setting to help you to identify your clients' perceptions of their own strengths and resources.

Now, if you haven't already done so, take a minute to follow the directions and complete all six boxes in the NSRI form.

There isn't any scoring to the NSRI. The NSRI is a tool that I developed with my clients in therapy years ago simply to have them tell me what strengths and resources they possess.

In Section One, here are some practical and useful things which many of my clients do have close friends, reliable transportation, a pet, internet access, stable living environments, uniforms and clothing, healthy food choices, a primary care physician, a source of income. Instead of looking at what's wrong and what's not there, I want to know from my clients what is there.

The second category is all about interaction with self and others. Do they perceive that they are able to solve problems, follow directions, give clear directions, work well in a team, work independently, listen well, express thoughts or feelings, create plans, develop creative options? Instead of focusing on what's wrong (how come you have difficulty with others or with yourself?), instead I'm looking for what's right. This is the most effective starting point for change.

Section Three focuses on education and job skills. It simply assesses my client's perception of the resources they bring to the table from an educational perspective: high school diploma or GED, military training, vocational or technical certificate, and a college degree or higher. Do they have a resume? Do they have management or supervisor experience? Have they done volunteer or charity work? Do they have a job history of more than six months? Do they have a job history of more than two years? Can they pass an alcohol or drug screening?

In Section Four, there are 24 options. I want them to choose six of those traits, which include creative, curious, open-minded, inquisitive, wise, brave, persistent, honest, high-energy, loving, kind, aware, a team-player, fair, a leader, forgiving, humble, careful, having impulse-control, appreciative, grateful, optimistic, humor, and spiritual.

I was talking to the vice president of the local chamber of commerce. One of her jobs is to help local employers find qualified employees. And she said to me, "If they have reliable transportation and can pass a drug screening, I can find anybody a job."

The fifth block includes things like cooking, sports, exercise, building things, music, arts and crafts, games and puzzles, singing, reading, writing stories or poems, dancing, travel, family time, community involvement, and religious services. And these things in and of themselves might even appear trivial to some. But the reality is, for the individuals who I work with, I can often find the solution to very complex problems based in the activities, and the personal interest and the abilities which they already possess.

In the sixth block, we're assessing social and situational supports: family members, community members, and so on. Nobody ever got well alone. People are social by nature. We do best when we have others to support us. King Solomon said it this way, "As iron sharpens iron, so one man sharpens another." And so I want my clients to put a mark next to any or all of the following who they think would be able to help them at this time: a mother, a father, a sister, a brother, a step-parent, a grandparent, another relative, a best friend, a close friend, new friends, a boss or supervisor, a co-worker, a religious leader, a neighbor, a support group, a mentor, a coach, a counselor, a therapist, a spouse, or a medical professional.

And the NSRI is not exhaustive. I don't purport to have a tool that measures all strengths, all resources, all personality traits, and all of the things that a person needs. You can adapt this to the people that you work with. Feel free to make it better and apply it to your particular situation. I've intentionally reduced the number of choices so that it would fit on the one page. As I meet with somebody whom I've never met before, it's my goal to move them quickly out of their state of pain or discomfort. It's far easier for me to do that by focusing on their strengths than their deficits. And this is tool that gives me the ability to measure and identify those strengths.

Chapter Four:

Leadership Charisma

When we think about charisma, we often wonder if it's something we possess. Chances are that your idea of an effective leader is predicated to some extent on perceptions of charisma. You might even wonder if you have the potential to develop charisma as a part of your leadership style.

Of course, there are those who actually exude charisma. Still, it is dangerous to limit an understanding of charisma to that role of a magnetic savior or a mystical and powerful communicator who is simply born with a gleam in the eye and a perfectly fitted suit. This mystical view of charisma comes from Webber, the first sociologist to define charisma as a function of leadership. He viewed it as an "endowment with divine grace."[21] I do not believe it is as mystical as Webber made it sound.

If you do a Google search for *charisma,* you'll find a lot of blogs; you'll find that there are a lot of books and a lot of self-help material purporting to teach charisma. One blog that I scanned in preparing this material was very practical, actually giving specific brand recommendations for clothing purchases so that the wearer could be more charismatic; it directed those who want to enhance their charisma to learn witty jokes and one-line platitudes.

But that's really rather a trivial understanding of charisma. Charisma is not about the clothing that one wears or the witty jokes they can tell. Charisma is actually about communication and connection. Specifically, charisma is about building rapport and enhancing cooperation. It is about connecting to other people.

---

21   Bernard M. Bass, Ruth Bass, and Bernard M. Bass, *The Bass Handbook of Leadership: Theory, Research, and Managerial Applications*, 4th ed. (New York: Free Press, 2008). 575.

Charisma without transformation is often short-lived. History is filled with business stories of charismatic leaders who look like the right person for the part but failed to create transformation. Enron, an energy company in the 1990's, was one of the biggest corporate failures of all time. The charismatic leaders of this company, Ken Lay and Jeffery Skilling, have even been called corporate cult leaders in professional business journals.[22] The corporate culture of Enron failed to utilize charisma to promote an ethical approach to business. Rather, it promoted an approach that saw the end as justifying the means. The story of Enron and its charismatic key management is a tragic story with many people suffering financial loss, and even suicide, as a result of the company's downfall.

Although Burns saw charismatic leadership as a hindrance to transformation, to some extent the debate over which of these two forms of leadership is better is a lot like trying to pick the most beautiful contestant at a beauty pageant. Some authors actually view charismatic leadership and Transformational Leadership as two sides of the same coin–in fact, charisma is noted by Bass as a frequent component of Transformational Leadership. Bass even notes that the charismatic leader is likely to be transformational, but it is possible—although unlikely—to be transformational without being charismatic.

Charisma can play a role in Transformational Leadership, helping us to transform others by improving esprit de corps. Charisma is one pathway to accomplishing what Randy Dobbs sees as an essential function of leadership: creating a shared vision, enthusiasm for being a part of that vision, and working together towards clearly defined collective goals.[23]

What is a healthy perspective on charisma and how can it be used to promote transformation? Bass identifies eight characteristics of the charismatic leader.[24] All of these can become a foundation for transformation when charismatic leaders utilize them within the context of an ethical framework, with an end desire to create a cadre of future transformational leaders rather than an agenda predicated on narcissism or grandiosity.

- Self-confidence

- Self-determination

---

22   Dennis Tourish and Naheed Vatcha, "Charismatic Leadership and Corporate Cultism at Enron: The Elimination of Dissent, the Promotion of Conformity and Organizational Collapse," *Leadership* 1, no. 4 (2005).

23   Dobbs.

24   Bass et al.

- Insight
- Freedom form internal conflict
- Eloquence and rhetoric
- Activity and energy level
- Self-sacrificial disposition
- Vision creation

Self-confidence:

Charismatic leaders have confidence in themselves, their ability to lead, and their ability to communicate this self-confidence to others.

Self-determination:

Now, at an unhealthy level this could be part of narcissism or even self-centeredness. But really, what we're looking at from a healthy perspective here is the ability to act autonomously.

Insight:

The ability to think outside of the box, the ability to operate in the grey areas, the ability to change perceptual positions and see things from a new or unique vantage point.

Freedom from internal conflict:

Now, all of us in our lives will experience some form of disharmony or internal conflict at one point or another. Really, what Bass is alluding to here is the idea of emotional intelligence, which is something we're going to spend an entire chapter discussing.

Eloquence and rhetoric:

Really an ability to communicate clearly to other people, both in written form as well as verbal form, and even non-verbal communication.

High energy level:

The ability to engage in numerous and strenuous activities, often for many hours, without appearing worn out or dispirited. Leadership is hard work.

Self-sacrificial disposition:

Looking out for the welfare of others. This certainly was not something that was present in the Enron case that I mentioned a while ago.

Ability to create vision:

The capacity to see beyond the present and into the future, and to see how we can bring the present into the future.

There's a book that I used years ago in counseling called *The Skilled Helper*. It was written by Gerard Egan, a professor at Loyola University of Chicago. In his conceptualization of the counseling process, he had three scenes: the present scene, the preferred scene, and the programmatic scene.

The present scene is of course where we are now. The preferred scene is where we would like to be—essentially, the vision. And that third scene in Egan's model, the programmatic scene, is what we're going to do in order to move there. The charismatic leader is able to see all three of these components–whether it's in business, family, coaching, mentoring, or any other endeavor where we're motivating and helping people.

To use charisma as a key to transformation, you have to ask yourself: "Which of these eight traits do I need to develop and practice?" Look over the eight characteristics listed above and ask yourself that question. Chances are pretty good you're strong in a couple of these, but you could use some practice in some of the other ones. For almost anything we do in life, hoping to do it well is usually the goal. This is no difference between developing charisma and learning to play golf or a musical instrument. Sure, some people seem to be born with natural aptitudes that make mastery easier. But even golf pros and Carnegie Hall musicians practice to become perfect.

As you identify the eight characteristics of charisma and evaluate your proficiency in these areas, ask yourself, "How can I practice?" Let me give you some examples. Let's say you have the need to practice self-confidence. What could you do to practice this, to step into a state of being confident in really any situation? It's amazing how the simple things that we can practice actually yield the best results. People who would like to be more self-confident and exude self-confidence are people who practice healthy posture. Our posture can communicate, on a non-verbal level, self-confidence.

Another thing you can do to practice self-confidence is you can take the strengths that you identified in Section 4 of the NSRI—we covered that in last chapter—and write those things, those attributes or characteristics that you possess that are your strengths and tape them on the bathroom mirror. The reason why I want you tape it to the bathroom mirror is it's the first thing you see in the morning usually and the last thing you see at the end of the day. And then, as you step out of your bathroom door in the morning, step out of the bathroom with intention, trying to manifest those strengths which you are already good at rather than trying to add to your repertoire or fixing what you perceive is wrong with you. When you, with intention, utilize those strengths that you identified in Section 4 of the NSRI, you'll actually be practicing self-confidence.

How do you practice developing eloquence and rhetoric? A lot of people really struggle with communication at a level that could be called eloquent or rhetoric that is clear. Well, here are two ideas to use if this is an area where you would like to improve your proficiency, where you would like to practice. Identify ten words that you have the greatest difficulty spelling or pronouncing. If eloquence and rhetoric is an area where you would like to improve, there are probably ten words that you use or that you commonly misspell or mispronounce that you can dedicate time to mastering. They might be words like entrepreneur, paradigm, and epitome, or even words like there, their, and they're. Identifying words that sometimes people have a difficult time with and practicing them so that you know how to spell them accurately in your written communication and pronounce them clearly in your verbal communication will help you to be more confident and eloquent. The pay-off of practicing just those ten words, which you stumble over currently, will last you the rest of your life. Like I said, it will improve your self-confidence, also.

Another way to develop or practice eloquence and rhetoric is to seek out opportunities to practice your public speaking. Practice makes perfect. They say that the most common phobia people experience is the fear of speaking in front of others. In my practice as a therapist, I actually have a lot of people come to me because they are afraid of public speaking. Experience is what helps make this natural, and it will improve your eloquence and your rhetoric in groups of all sizes. So rather than turning down an opportunity to make a presentation, seize any opportunity you have to practice public speaking.

How do you practice improving your activity and energy levels? What can you do to become a more energetic person in your leadership? It may sound simple or even trite, but exercise and eat right. I'm amazed at how many people complain of low energy levels and then when I ask them what they had for lunch or what they had for breakfast, I discover that they're eating a diet of simple carbohydrates—doughnuts for breakfast. Sugar results in a burst of energy and then periods of sluggishness and fatigue. Simple dietary changes can actually make a huge difference to a person's energy level. And of course the carbs that we should be eating are those that will sustain our energy level, and those are complex carbohydrates like those found in beans, zucchini, lentils, and whole grains.

And then of course, the way to increase our activity level is to participate in daily activity. It really is a matter of use it or lose it. Exercise is an important part of every leader's day. A person doesn't have to join the gym, or join a Zumba class, or participate in a structured exercise program in order to increase their physical activity and increase their energy levels. Simply walking does it. One of the great things about the current era is that we all have a smart phone (or at least most of us do). You can go to the app store on your smart phone, and you can actually download a pedometer application. I always give this suggestion to people who need to increase their energy level. Use the smart phone pedometer app and measure your steps each day, taking more steps today than yesterday, more steps tomorrow than today, and increasing your steps to 10,000 steps each day. Although these ideas are simple and don't really seem to be related to charisma, when we look at them independently, we can see that they are. Each of these eight areas can be practiced, and you can develop characteristics of charisma through practical rehearsal that reinforces each of these eight areas.

Cooperation and Teamwork

Back in the early 2000's an email was circulating that told a remarkable story from the Special Olympics. Like a lot things on the Internet, the email embellished the story a little from an event that actually did happen in 1976. But here's the Internet version of the story:

A few years ago, at the Seattle Special Olympics, nine contestants, all physically or mentally disabled, assembled at the starting line for the 100-yard dash. At the gun, they all started out, not exactly in a dash, but with relish to run the race and finish and win.

All, that is, except one little boy who stumbled right out of the line on the asphalt, he tumbled over a couple of times, and began to cry. The other eight heard the boy cry.

They slowed down and looked back. Then they all turned around and went back. Every single one of them. One girl with Down's Syndrome bent down and kissed him and said, "This will make it better." Then all nine linked arms and walked together to the finish line. Everyone in the stadium stood still, and the cheering went on for several minutes. People who were there are still telling the story.

Another new story has recently been floating around the internet, this one from January of 2013. It shows a spirit of cooperation, of camaraderie, and being able to build rapport through genuine caring of another person. The new story said this:

> It's hard not to be a little cynical about the sporting world. The story of long distance runner Iván Fernández Anaya may serve as a welcome antidote. The Spanish runner, who trains in the Basque capital of Vitoria-Gasteiz, has become something of a cult hero for a kind gesture that helped an opponent win a race.
>
> Fernández Anaya was trailing behind Olympic bronze medalist Abel Mutai during a cross-country race in Burlada, Navarra. Mutai was leading comfortably until he pulled up 10 to 20 meters short of the finish line thinking the race was already over. Instead of passing Mutai, Fernández Anaya slowed down and told Mutai to keep running. Since they didn't speak a common language, the Basque runner gestured frantically at Mutai who went on to win the race.
>
> "I didn't deserve to win it," Fernández Anaya told El País. "I did what I had to do. He was the rightful winner. He created a gap that I couldn't have closed if he hadn't made a mistake. As soon as I saw he was stopping, I knew I wasn't going to pass him."
>
> Fernández Anaya's actions may not have earned him the win, but they did earn him many new fans.

In Chapter One, I said that everything I learned about leadership, I learned in therapy. My approach to therapy is one that's been described as the cooperation principle. In therapy, I learned that being the expert—in other words, depending on charisma alone—did not produce sufficient change. And in therapy, I learned that behaviorism, which really is a transactional approach to leadership, was rather limited. My goal with my clients is to help them to change by being with them, attending to them and caring about them.

I view myself as a coach doing something *with* them rather than transactionally or charismatically doing something *to* them.

The cooperation principle easily applies, outside of therapy, to any endeavor where we're interacting with others, and this is a hallmark of transformational leaders. Dobbs alludes to this cooperation principle in his description of the manager vs. the leader. He writes, "Managers usually establish a one-team process in which they control the team to their benefit and desires. Leaders who build teams with few mandates know that teams only progress if they are allowed to experiment and grow at varied rates, just as a family grows and changes over time."[25]

Cooperation is the key to this aspect of leadership development. The cooperation principle describes how people interact. Psycholinguist Paul Grice introduced this idea in the context of linguistics: "Make your contributions such as it is required, at the stage at which it occurs, by the accepted purpose or direction of the talk exchange in which you are engaged."[26]

The summary of the principles of Paul Grice yields four maxims for conversation, referred to as Grice's Maxims. In understanding Grice's Maxims, we can understand how everyday communication with those around us can enhance cooperation. Although written like a prescription, these are not just prescriptive verbal communications, but are designed to facilitate cooperation at all levels of communication. And these really aren't things we actually even need to strive to do. According to Grice, they are actually ingrained into our communication intergenerationally from thousands of years of human development.

Grice's Four Maxims can be expressed this way:

The maxim of quantity:
Provide no more nor less than the communication requires.

The maxim of quality:
Offer communication based on fact, honesty, and empiricism.

The maxim of relation:
Be relevant.

The maxim of manner:
Be clear and brief.

---

25   Dobbs.

26   H. P. Grice, *Studies in the Way of Words* (Cambridge, Mass.: Harvard University Press, 1989).

The value of knowing Grice's Maxims is that it gives us a model for checking our communication for clarity and cooperation. It is essentially one form of direct or even assertive communication. I've seen leaders fail when these maxims were not followed. I've seen leaders fail to observe the maxim of quantity and overwhelm followers. I've also seen the converse, where a leader didn't provide sufficient information, failing to adhere to the maxim of quantity in their communication.

As one who has done a fair number of employee interviews, I've seen otherwise qualified candidates blow the position because their communication with either me or another interviewer failed to adhere to the maxim of quantity, providing far more information than we ever wanted to know, essentially disqualifying them for the position. And I've seen the converse: not providing enough quantity, essentially answering yes or no to an open-ended question.

When the maxim of relation is discarded, many projects lose focus and meetings can become less than productive or even counter-productive. Have you ever been to a scheduled meeting where you were going to discuss one topic but somebody introduced an unrelated topic alongside of the planned topic, and all of the momentum and energy was lost?

Similarly, whenever the maxim of manner is ignored, obscurity and ambiguity are the results. The maxim of manner discusses, of course, clarity and brevity.

You can fail to promote cooperation in conversations by violating these expected conversational maxims. In knowing what Grice's conversational maxims are, we know what's expected of us in creating two-way communication. We've all met a boss or a co-worker who failed at effective communication. And they usually do it because they violate one of these conversational maxims. They can violate these conversational maxims with deception, by opting out, or choosing not to participate, or by changing topic, or by providing too much or too little information and being ambiguous. And none of those things foster cooperation. The idea of creating cooperation really is simple. The idea is create healthy conversations. Grice's maxims tell us both what healthy conversations and communications are composed of and what our expectations in communication truly are.

Rapport

Rapport is essential. Rapport is about being in sync with somebody else. It's an exchange with another that occurs not only verbally, but multi-sensorialy. It's the art of interpersonal connection. Sociologists tell us that we make important judgments about people we meet within the first seven seconds of interacting with them.

Now, as a therapist, I was taught that building rapport was essential, and I was actually taught an acronym for the things that would communicate rapport with somebody who is in my office. And the acronym was SOLER:

- **S**it down

- have **O**pen body posture

- **L**ean forward

- make **E**ye contact

- **R**elax

That acronym is something simple. But it's actually helped me in situations where I've met somebody new and maybe I was nervous about meeting them or knew they were nervous about meeting me. I was able to either put them at ease or control my own anxiety by utilizing this acronym that I learned in graduate school.

There are other ways though that we can build rapport as a leader. One of those ways is through reciprocity. This might include gifts, or tokens, or even assisting or helping another person in an effort to elicit the return of a favor. Now, the idea here is simply to cause a state of reciprocity without causing a sense of obligation on the part of the other person. So there's definitely some balance here. For example, if I was a sales person and I had a client who I was attempting to sell products to, I probably wouldn't give them a gold watch worth $10,000.00. But I might give them corporate key chains or sticky notepads with our corporate logo on it or even with their corporate logo on it.

Commonality is another way to develop rapport with individuals. Look for common ground. Whenever I am meeting with somebody for the first time, I will Google them and find out all I can about them. I'll check out their LinkedIn profile and their Facebook page. I'll even see some of the things they've written. It's likely that some post on the Internet unrelated to their work or vocation will express some of the shared interest that we might have.

And I can look for opportunities then to connect through commonality with somebody.

Cognitive dissonance is another way develop rapport. The idea with cognitive dissonance is that people dislike a situation where there is discomfort or dissatisfaction. And so, in my interactions with somebody, I could express a level of discomfort, dissatisfaction, or even irritation in an attempt to elicit an action that will cause the other person to take action to minimize the discomfort. In other words, with intention, I'm creating cognitive dissonance that releases their expression of empathy. If somebody is manifesting empathy towards me, kind of like reciprocity, they can go towards building rapport. Now, again, with reciprocity and cognitive dissonance, we could use these unethically and manipulate individuals. But they can also be a part of building rapport with an individual in a healthy context as well.

I think one of the easiest ways to build rapport as a leader is to be likable, to be nice. Niceness counts. Say something kind to somebody else, smile.

Another way to build rapport is to be approachable. Let me share a story from my own personal experience years ago when I was working as a therapist at an in-patient adolescent psychiatric facility.

I was actually a new therapist. I had graduated with my bachelor's degree and my master's degree, and I had a professional membership in a professional association, so they mailed me an awesome certificate. I was actually very proud of those accomplishments. Because I was very proud of those accomplishments in my office, in that first job, I hung those diplomas on the wall, and I hung my certificate of membership next to my diplomas on the wall. Then a kid came into my office. He was anxious, and I was his case manager. When I invited him to share with me some of the things that he was thinking of, he just kind of looked frustrated at me—I was wearing a tie, and my diplomas were on the wall—and he said, "I don't think you'll understand. You're not like me at all."

What is interesting is I had read his history in his chart, and I had actually met him during his intake evaluation and also heard the treatment team discuss their prior interactions with him. In many ways, his experiences in life actually mirrored some of my own experiences in. I knew that I was actually far more like him than he would ever understand. But there were things in my environment that did not invite rapport. Those diplomas hanging on the wall were things that he didn't have. That tie was something he didn't relate to. Remember, I was working with kids in a residential treatment facility.

But I was a new therapist and, perhaps self-conscious of being young myself, wanted to appear professional, so I wore a tie to work everyday. That particular kid never did open up to me, but he taught me something very important about rapport that day.

When I got done with work, I took off my tie. I actually went to the mall and bought some more casual clothes that did not require a tie. I also stopped at the art store at the mall. There was a store at the mall that sold art, pictures, cute sayings, and those sorts of things. I bought a couple of them, one of them I still have to this day. It was a picture of Winnie the Pooh, and Winnie the Pooh was stuck in the honey tree. And Christopher Robin and Eeyore and all of the other characters from the Pooh cartoon were trying to pull Winnie the Pooh out of the honey tree, and it said at the bottom: "It all comes from loving honey too much." I thought to myself, "Wow, as an addiction counselor, this is actually a perfect poster for my office wall." Another poster that was there on the shop was a poster of Robert Folghum's book *Everything I Needed To Know I Learned In Kindergarten.* It had some sayings from that book all over, written out in an artistic way. And so I bought those and I had them framed.

The next day, I went back to my office with a sweater instead of a tie, and I took my diplomas down off the wall, and I hung the Winnie the Pooh and the Robert Fulghum poster up the wall where my diplomas were. By the way, I took those diplomas home. I didn't even leave them in my office. I shoved them under the bed. And if you actually come over my house today, you'll actually find my diplomas from all of my various education experiences literally in frames under the bed in my master bedroom. Even though I was never able to develop rapport with that particular kid, since that time, other people have come into my office and they haven't seen anything in my office that would indicate to them that they would not be able to open up to me, share honestly, and take a risk.

What I've been talking about to some extent here is really about suspending ego—putting other people first and building rapport by recognizing the importance of suspending our own egos.

Another great way to build rapport is simply to validate people. A few years ago on the Internet there was an excellent short film put out about the importance of validation. It was very creative. It was about a mall employee whose job is to validate parking stamps. While doing that, he also told people how wonderful they were, offering genuine validation. People love the feeling of being validated, and the short story is really pretty cute. Think back to when you were in kindergarten; maybe you got gold stars by your name. The gold stars weren't worth anything: you couldn't take them home. In fact, they were actually made out of paper and glue. And yet, for some reason we loved earning gold stars. It meant that somebody recognized us for our work. If you want to build rapport with a team, recognize the valuable contributions that they make. Validate people.

(If you want to see the short film, *Validation,* it is posted on YouTube and has over 8 million views: http://youtu.be/Cbk980jV7Ao)

Another way to build rapport is to create artificial time constraints. If we're in a new conversation or we're in a conversation with somebody where we may lose momentum, one of the things we can do is we can predetermine a time period for a meeting with an individual so that way we don't run out of momentum and end up with that twenty-minute lull.

Research shows that some other ways of building rapport come from a technique called Matching or Matching and Mirroring. We can match a person's body language. If they are sitting in a formal posture with us, we can join them in that formal posture. If they're sitting in a relaxed posture, we can join them in that relaxed posture. If they are open in their body language, we can be open. If they closed in their body language, we can build rapport with them by letting them know it's okay to be closed at the moment by closing off ourselves a little bit also. Of course, this must be done carefully so as to not appear mocking or disrespectful.

We can also match language. In one of the previous chapters I shared with you *The Nongard Assessment of Primary Representational Systems.* We can intentionally choose to communicate with individuals utilizing their primary representational system or learning style. If we have an auditory person, we communicate with auditory language. When we have a visual person, we communicate with visual imagery and visual language. We have a kinesthetic person, we communicate with kinesthetic language.

And then, another way of matching and mirroring is to match and mirror paralanguage. This would be the rate, the volume, the pitch. And by matching a person, we can develop a state of being in sync with them.

Failing all else, simply breathe in sync with the person you are talking to. Groups that breathe together often develop a sense of group identity and rapport; this is one purpose for songs, chanting, and shouting slogans in religious and political meetings. (The Latin word *conspiracy* literally means "breathing together.") And when we develop this level of rapport with individuals, we can find ourselves in a position to easily lead other people into transformation and transition.

In the next couple of chapters, I'm going to discussing emotional intelligence and social intelligence: important concepts as we try to make the study of Transformational Leadership something that's practical for you in the work that you do with the individuals that are important to you.

Chapter Five:

Emotional Intelligence

How smart are you? I was actually never really good at math, and I am a lousy speller. These two things have, despite my now having a master's degree and a doctorate, got me down on occasion. My son, on the other hand, is a great speller. He even got a 35 on the English portion of the ACT and an overall score of 33. That means only about 1% of the test-takers on a national level scored higher than he did. Although I don't remember my ACT scores, I'm pretty sure they weren't that high. Sometimes he corrects my spelling, or solves a math problem at the grocery store or computes miles per gallon at a gas station faster than me. And I'm glad he is smart but occasionally, I feel like I'm not as smart as I would have hoped.

Do you ever wonder if you're not as smart as others? Well, I have great news if you're in the same boat as I am. First, you can still be a leader. In a meta-analysis by Judge, Colbert, and Ilies, they found that "the relationship between intelligence and leadership is considerably lower than previously thought."[27] According to a synthesis of the data, factors such "the leader's stress level and the leader's directiveness moderated the intelligence-leadership relationship." Essentially, they concluded that there is more than one way to measure smart beyond 'pencil and paper' measures of intelligence.

Second, the writings of Howard Gardner at Yale University help us to understand that intelligence can be measured in many different ways—not just in math, grammar, and analogy puzzles as standardized tests do. For Gardner, intelligence is the ability to create an effective product or offer a service that's

---

27   T. A. Judge, A. E. Colbert, and R. Ilies, "Intelligence and Leadership: A Quantitative Review and Test of Theoretical Propositions," *J Appl Psychol* 89, no. 3 (2004).

valued in a culture. Intelligence, according to Gardner, is a set of skills that make it possible for a person to solve problems in life. Gardner views intelligence as the potential for finding or creating solutions to problems which involve gathering knowledge.[28] It's not just about math or spelling. Gardner proposed actually nine different ways to be intelligent:

- Linguistic Intelligence

- Logical/Mathematical Intelligence

- Musical Rhythmic Intelligence

- Bodily/Kinesthetic Intelligence

- Spatial Intelligence

- Naturalistic Intelligence

- Intrapersonal Intelligence

- Interpersonal Intelligence

- Existential Intelligence

Linguistic intelligence might include writing, speaking, or really anything that has to do with language and the expression of that language.

The second way of looking at intelligence is logical/mathematical intelligence. Of course, we are familiar with that from standardized testing.

Gardner also talks about a musical and rhythmic intelligence, recognition of patterns, and the ability to manipulate sound. Musicians and effective public speakers may rely on this intelligence.

The fourth intelligence Gardner looks at is a bodily or kinesthetic intelligence. In this type of intelligence a person produces with his body and this could be anything from crafts to athletics.

The fifth kind of intelligence is spatial intelligence. Pilots, rocket scientists, and engineers, for example, need good spatial intelligence.

The sixth type of intelligence is naturalistic intelligence. Somebody who is smart from a nature perspective. An example of this might be an agricultural worker or even a good friend of mine who is a herpetologist.

---

28   "Howard Gardner's Multiple Intelligences Theory", Public Boradcasting Service http://www.pbs.org/wnet/gperf/education/ed_mi_overview.html (accessed March 8, 2014).

Intrapersonal intelligence is the intelligence really that's based on the idea of self-awareness.

Number eight according to Gardner is interpersonal intelligence. This is about connectedness to others and the ability to interact well.

And number nine is existential intelligence. Intelligence related to life, death, philosophy.

In Gardner's conceptualization, number 7 (intrapersonal intelligence) and number 8 (interpersonal intelligence) are going to join to form the basis for our understanding of both emotional intelligence in this chapter and social intelligence in the next chapter. Based at least to some extent on the ideas of multiple intelligences in Gardner's work, these two expressions of intelligence—emotional intelligence and social intelligence—have changed the face of many leadership training programs.

Although both of these concepts are, to some extent, components of Gardner's conceptualization, they've been popularized recently by the best-selling writings of Dr. Daniel Goleman. He's a licensed psychologist and two-time Pulitzer Prize nominee. Dr. Daniel Goleman's work in social intelligence and emotional intelligence has been largely embraced by corporate training programs.

Critics of both emotional intelligence and social intelligence have criticized these concepts as really identifying abilities rather than intelligences, yet recent research has actually demonstrated the value of both of these in leadership practice.[29]

Another criticism of emotional intelligence is that it really hasn't been differentiated from personality traits plus I.Q. or from the multiplicity of definitions that make validating the concept and endeavors of emotional intelligence practical. But proponents of emotional intelligence as a measured intelligence actually provide much greater support for emotional intelligence than critics usually report.[30] Emotional intelligence, whether viewed as a form of intelligence or an ability, is a powerful concept in both intrapersonal and interpersonal relationships.

Emotional intelligence is defined as the capacity to be aware of controlling and expressing one's emotions, along with the capacity to handle interpersonal relationships judiciously and empathetically.

29   Cary Cherniss et al., "Emotional Intelligence: What Does the Research Really Indicate?," *Educational Psychologist* 41, no. 4 (2006).

30   Ibid.

Goleman actually defines four components in his book on emotional intelligence:

- Self-Awareness
- Self-Management
- Empathy
- Skilled Relationships

The first is a state of self-awareness—knowing why we feel what we feel, and being able to identify within ourselves what the purpose or value of those feelings are.

The second component of emotional intelligence according to Goleman is self-management—the ability to effectively handle distressing emotions, but even more importantly, the ability to generate positive emotion.

Empathy is the third component. It's really about knowing how other people feel. This is what fosters a connection. Remember in one of our earlier chapters I referred to counseling and therapy as belly-button-to-belly-button communication. Being able to communicate on an empathetic level is the heart of many different professions that mentor, teach, and counsel people—from pastors to teachers to mentors in the traditional business context.

And the fourth element of emotional intelligence identified by Goleman is skilled relationships—combining all of these abilities and attributes in a meaningful way.

These four components have the potential to create transformation when leaders developed within each of these areas.

My experience has been that I've seen highly intelligent and qualified leaders fail to create transformation when they lack empathy or the ability to generate positive emotions. At the same time, I've seen leaders with minimal intellect rise above their peer networks, based in large part on manifesting emotional intelligence.

There are some who have claimed that emotional intelligence is the greatest predictor of success in life. That's actually kind of a grandiose claim, and I refer to that type of a claim as a nominalization. It really is meaningless. In other words, what is 'success' and what is 'greatness'? So even though meaningless claims, such as emotional intelligence is the greatest predictor of success of life, aren't particularly useful to us, there has been enough research into the utility of emotional intelligence to demonstrate that *in a number of areas,* emotional intelligence is a predictor of success. These specific areas of life can correlate with leadership. These areas of correlation include academic performance and school grades, reductions in deviancy, pro-social and positive behaviors, and leadership within organizational behavior.[31]

Sometimes people have asked, "What does a person with high-level of emotional intelligence look like?' Let me share for you a composite picture:

The high E.I. individual, most centrally, can better perceive emotions, use them in thought, understand their meanings, and manage emotions better than others. So emotional problems likely require less cognitive effort for this individual. The person also tends to be somewhat higher in verbal, social, and other intelligence–particularly if the individual scored higher in the Understanding Emotions portion of emotional intelligence. This individual tends to be more open and agreeable than others. The high E.I. person is drawn to occupations that involve social interactions, such as teaching, counseling, more than to occupations involving clerical or administrative tasks. The high E.I. individuals relative to others is less apt to engage in problem be-haviors and avoid self-destructive negative behaviors, such as smoking, drinking, drug abuse, and violent episodes. The high E.I. person is more likely to have possessions of sentimental attachment around the home. And they have more positive social interactions, particularly if the individual scored highly on emotional management. Such indi-viduals may also be more adept at describing motivational goals, aims, and missions.[32]

That may be the composite picture of what research shows a high emotional intelligence individual to be like. But in my own mind, it's also a composite picture of what effective transformational leaders look like.

So here's a question for you: How can you develop your emotional intelligence? If we go back to Chapter One, you will recall that the theory of positive psychology states that you already possess within you many of the resources necessary for manifesting high levels of emotional intelligence.

Let's look at the four areas that Goleman identified, the first being

---

31   Galit Meisler and Eran Vigoda-Gadot, "Perceived Organizational Politics, Emotional Intelligence and Work Outcomes: Empirical Exploration of Direct and Indirect Effects," *Personnel Review* 43, no. 1 (2014).

32   John Mayer, Peter Salovey, and David Caruso, "Emotional Intelligence: Theory, Findings, and Implications," *Psychological Inquiry* 15, no. 3 (2004). 210.

self-awareness. This is the capacity to find one's self apart from situations, apart from other people, or apart from temporary distress. This is why it's so important in leadership. A leader who takes personally the temporal difficulties of any situation is likely to become enmeshed in that and fail to see beyond the crisis to a resolution.

Self-Awareness Strategies

Self-awareness can be enhanced in many different ways. Linguistics actually gives us four power words for self-awareness, and those power words are: notice, see, realize, and aware. These are power words in developing self-awareness because the meaning we give to these words leads to self-awareness. They help us experiences ourselves in context of something larger than ourselves. I always suggest to people that they write those four words down on an index card:

- notice

- see

- realize

•, aware

I further encourage my clients to, any time they find themselves in any type of difficult situation or stressful experience, ask themselves, "What do I notice? What do I see? What do I realize? And what am I aware of?" This simple practice can go a long way in helping to create a sense of self-awareness.

A baby cries when the parent leaves peripheral vision because a baby is unaware that even if a parent can't be seen, the parent still remains present. Words like *notice, see, realize,* and *aware* ask us to start paying attention to the context of any situation, not just the experience of a situation.

Another way to generate self-awareness is to create a daily exercise. At the end of each day, take time to ask yourself: "What's one thing I noticed today? What's one thing that I saw was different? What global realization did the day bring? And how has my awareness changed as the result of these reflections?"

Now, if you just read this assignment and move on from here through the rest of the book, this assignment probably won't have much value. But I'm going to give an assignment right here, right now, for you to work on throughout the next week. Write those words on a note card. At the end of each day, before you close your eyes and drift into sleep, take four minutes and answer each of those questions. Do it each and everyday for the next seven days. When you do that, the value of those power words will then become evident to you, and it's probably something you're going to continue to do long after the assignment is over.

The next strategy for self-awareness is to take advantage of the many re-sources, many of them online, which can help you to know yourself, better. You can simply Google "emotional intelligence test," and you can use any of those to find out more about yourself. There are exercises that identify indi-vidual strengths, much like the NSRI in the previous chapter. There are online resources to identify your spiritual gifts and personality traits. All of these things can help you to become more aware of yourself.

Bill Hendricks is the author of a book called *The Person Called You*. He is the director of the Giftedness Center in Dallas, Texas. For more than 20 years he's been helping people to answer these questions:

- Why are you here?

- Why do you matter?

- What you should do with your life?

Hendricks says that the key is found in harnessing the power of gift-edness. This is approach really is unique. It's based on exploring one's own life story. In some ways Bill's work at the Giftedness Center really parallels Solution-Focused Brief Therapy, an approach that I've used that's known for its exception-seeking questions. Instead of looking at what's wrong or why the problem is so difficult, the exception question asks a person who is struggling with a problem to look back and identify a time when normally they would have manifested the same problem, but for some reason didn't.

For example, somebody who is struggling with drinking everyday might look back and find a time when there was a weekend a few months back, when they attended their child's college graduation or whatever event it was, when for some reason they just didn't drink. And by analyzing the factors present in that exceptional event, clients in counseling can explore the exception to the problem and identify the unique strengths that can be found already within themselves to create desired change.

Another strategy for self-awareness is to literally pay attention to you. A few moments of relaxation can help you take a break from the stress of the day or the business of study. But by taking a minute to physically be aware of yourself on both the physical and emotional level, you can increase self-awareness.

In my work in counseling, I work with a lot of people who are stressed. And often they are carrying the tension of the day some place in their body. But until I ask them to be aware of it, they often aren't aware that they have been storing that stress or tension there. Likewise, some of my clients have spent so much time in anxiety and depression, that until I ask them to be aware of other emotions, they really weren't aware of how depressed or how anxious they were.

At any time we can step outside of the stress of the day and take a moment to relax and reflect. We can actually ease ourselves into a state where we can observe ourselves, both on an emotional and physical level.

Strategies Self-Management and Creating Positive Emotions

Self-management is not just developing impulse-control to stop unwanted thoughts or behaviors. A leader needs to practice and hone an ability not only to stop unwanted thoughts or behavior, but more importantly, to step into positive emotions. This is really important because this skill, being able to create positive emotions, accomplishes two things. One, it keeps a leader from becoming enmeshed in group think or group negativity. And second, it empowers a leader to take control internally even when external things cannot be controlled. (By the way, practicing self-management models to others in crisis that it is possible to change subjective feelings.)

This all reminds me of an expression I learned many years ago: "You have the same pants to get glad in that you have to get mad in." But on an even more profound level, you actually have the ability anytime to elicit a positive state or any state, regardless of any external situation or experience. In counseling, I would often use this concept to move people from depression to satisfaction, or from anxiety to calm. I used a more remarkable application when I worked with drug offenders who associated positive feelings with the illegal act of getting high. To demonstrate for them the extent of their own ability to self-manage states that they desired without criminal behavior, I would take them to a process of creating all of the states they associated with being high but without ever touching any drugs. Now, think about the power in that. My clients believed they needed something outside of them to produce certain feelings that they desired—cocaine, alcohol, marijuana, and any other illegal drugs of abuse. But in a short time, I was able to help them recognize that at any time and any place, they have the capacity within themselves to produce those states apart from the illegal drugs or other problematic behavior.

Now, in this context, the word "state" means far more than just an emotion. It's an emotion in physiology, awareness, and experience. It's not just thinking about something, but fully associating into that state.

For example, think about the last time you were really angry. Chances are you were totally involved in the experience of anger. You probably felt strong emotion, but you probably also had a strong physiology with tensed muscles– and depending on the anger level, other physical sensations of the emotion. The state of anger can go beyond the feeling or even a physical sensation. It can permeate every aspect of our being.

As a therapist, I've worked with a lot of anger management clients over the years, and what I am about to say is the simplest realization. It is also the most profound:

We have the ability to change to any state
at any time and for any reason.

Now think about a state that can be a resource to you as you study this course, as you participate in this course on Transformational Leadership. Would it be the state of patience, or a state of curiosity, or of determination? Identify a resource state that you think might be useful to you as you study this material by whatever single word you might call it–curiosity, patience, determination, and learning.

Read through this process and then practice it:

Now, sit up in your chair. Put your shoulders back for a moment and close your eyes. As you close your eyes, think about the word that you picked to describe the resource state that would be most valuable to you. As you breathe in and out, associate into this state. What I mean by that is allow yourself to remember what that state felt like in the past when you experienced it, and bring your memory of this experience into the present. By associating into that state—I mean with every breath in and every breath out—breathe in learning, or breathe in curiosity, or breathe out determination, breathe out patience. Notice your mind and your body associating. Can you sense that?

Now, what we're going to do—continue to keep your eyes closed. Let's call your experience right now in creating this resource state a Level 1. With each breath, increase your experience of this resource state, allowing yourself to be filled with confidence, curiosity, determination, or whatever other word you used to describe that resource state. And as you breathe in and out, notice that Level 1 has moved to a higher level of awareness of this resource state, maybe even to a Level 4 or 5 or 6. You're doing great. Noticing your body, noticing your mind and your spirit moving to an even higher level. Feeling at a Level 7, Level 8, a Level 9, all the way to the highest level, a Level 10. Now, perfect. Open your eyes. Open your eyes and take in a breath. And when you take in a breath, notice you are what you have set out to create. You created more than just a positive emotion; you've become that which you identified as being valuable to you. This is really the art of self- management.

Empathy Strategies

When I was working on my master's degree, I actually took a course in the Counseling Program on Advanced Accurate Empathy, which at times struck me as a little bit silly. After all we were counseling students; why wouldn't we have empathy already? But of all the courses I took in graduate school, it was perhaps one of the most valuable courses. My emotional intelligence was enhanced by practicing with intention the art of empathy. I've always been one who has felt naturally empathetic. Learning to intentionally increase my awareness in practice during this course has really served me throughout my professional career.

As you expand your repertoire of strategies to practice increasing your emotional intelligence, intentionally being aware of others, practicing your non-verbal interpretation of communication, and using intuition to get a feel for people or all aspects of developing empathy that can be useful, consider this exercise in our busy world. Pick out a few hours of any day and decide to devote it to empathy. Make this a homework assignment you give yourself. Turn off your cell phone, step aside from Twitter or Facebook, and go out into the world uninterrupted and just observe people. Be with them. But go beyond observing them; make guesses as to what people are feeling. Choose to interact with some of those people. Demonstrate compassion. And with intention, watch and wonder about others, wonder what their experience is. This is actually a fun homework assignment or exercise to do, but it's also a great way to develop empathy through an intentional practice.

Skilled Relationship Strategies

Goleman's fourth characteristic of emotional intelligence involves synthesizing the other components to create skilled relationships. By combining these abilities and attributes in a meaningful way to navigate relationships, we create depth and establish trust. This is core leadership task. Self-awareness leads to healthy boundaries. Creating positive emotions and resource states can place you in a leadership capacity. Finally, practicing empathy contributes to creating interpersonal harmony.

On a very practical level, there are other things we can do to create and navigate relationships. A basic strategy of assertiveness communication is one excellent way to do this. So many times we react to others either aggressively. At other times, because we don't want to engage in any controversies, we respond passively. Or sometimes we think we can get away with passive-aggressive communication. And other people do sometimes get their way with aggressive, or passive, or passive-aggressive communication. The most effective way to be a leader in the area of relationships is to be assertive.

The basic formula sentence for assertiveness is:

"I feel / want / need _____."

I teach this to every client who comes in my office:

"I feel / want / need _____." (By the way, the period is important.)

I asked my clients to, with intention, practice this consciously each day. I ask them to use this formula at least once a day in their communication with their boss, co-worker, sibling, next-door neighbor, spouse, child, or parent. Implementing this strategy can help them to develop skilled relationships.

Chapter Six:

Social Intelligence

Social intelligence is another form of intelligence that leadership training programs have embraced and recognized as important. In leadership, motivation is often the mechanism of organizational energy, and motivation stems from social interaction. Leaders who understand social intelligence are able to effectively navigate complex social relationships and environments. Any time leaders are interacting with others, whether one-on-one in small or large groups, or even on a national and international level, complex relationships and navigating these interdependencies can determine outcomes in powerful ways.

To some extent, I'm reminded of the Butterfly Effect in Chaos Theory that says, "Even the small fluttering of a butterfly wing has the potential to stir up a hurricane somewhere else in the world." For some reason, I've always been fascinated by movies and stories related to time travel, and the Butterfly Effect is a common theme in these movies, where one event is determined by some seeming unrelated prior event.

Social intelligence essentially recognizes that human relationships are complex and interdependent.[33] Leaders must navigate these relationships with social intelligence, or the pathway of effective leadership can get complicated. One action can have a great impact on another event, even over time and space.

---

33   Daniel Goleman, *Social Intelligence: The New Science of Human Relationships* (New York: Bantam Books, 2006).

Social intelligence includes a number of different factors, including:

- Creating rapport

- Getting along well with others

- Fostering cooperation

- Situational awareness

- Judicious power

- Appropriate social interaction

There are five key dimensions that are often the descriptive framework for social intelligence. This is represented by the acronym SPACE:

- Situational Awareness

- Presence

- Authenticity

- Clarity

- Empathy

The S is for situational awareness--the ability to read situations and un-derstand the influences of behavior, and to choose the most successful strategy in any given situation. This is really when the Butterfly Effect comes into play. Social intelligence involves understanding how one seemingly minor element of a social network can have tremendous impact in another part of a social network.

The P is about presence. Presence is a consciousness of how others perceive you. For example, are you perceived with confidence, respect, and self-worth? It also has to do with whether or not you exude those attributes and qualities that you want others to perceive in you.

Authenticity is the A. It's about creating a context for the perception of integrity, honesty, empathy, and connection. These are the basis of leadership that truly transforms.

The C stands for clarity. We're talking about the social use of language and non-verbal communication to persuade others through the communication of ideas. In Transformational Leadership, this is really a contributing factor to gaining vision buy-in. If we want others to adopt our ideas as their own ideas, not simply because it's a means to an end, but because it's actually what's best for them. Clarity is one of those resources that are going to be essential.

And of course, the E stands for empathy—a connectedness to others that motivates them to work together for a greater good. Once again it's present in social intelligence just like it is in emotional intelligence.

Examples of Social Intelligence

Now, let me give you some examples of social intelligence. These are hypothetical examples, but I want to share with you a couple of examples just so you can see what we're really talking about when we speak of social intelligence. Here's an example of social intelligence in the context of negotiation:

Bob's been the president of a privately-held manufacturing company owned by a family that is not necessarily supportive of his financial goals. Although Bob has increased his sale volume, costs have risen. And to allow capital investment to procure more efficient machinery, the long-term prospect for success in a competitive industry is really pretty bleak. Bob's made his case on numerous occasions to the family patriarch who owns the company, but he's been rejected. Because of recent in changes in tax laws, purchasing new equipment this year has significant advantages over waiting another year or more. The board is meeting to consider this recommendation. However, the board is controlled by the family patriarch, who squashed this request in the past. It's also controlled by his two sons, one of whom is apathetic but has his father's ear, and the other son who's not a skilled business person, simply rubber stamping any decisions his father makes. This is a family-run business, and although Bob was appointed president because of his business credentials and operations experience, he's never been given the political power to get done what really needs in to be done in the long term.

In the past, Bob has always approached these negotiations with disdain for the family members whom he views as unqualified and with a little bit of resentment because the patriarch has not yielded to his expertise or relinquished any political power despite giving him the title of president. Bob has also used avoidance as a technique, never engaging with the family on a personal level, almost always declining social invitations and opportunities for engagement. Bob has done this because he felt the need to always be the professional, believing somebody needed to be the businessman in the room. Bob now recognizes that this next board meeting will make or break the business. After hours of preparing facts, charts, spread sheets, and a power point presentation, he actually deletes all of his power point slides and decides to come up with a new approach.

The day of board meeting, Bob opens the meeting with a short slide show, showing pictures of patriarch, the sons who run the business, and their children. He also shows slides of the family using the commercial products that they manufacture. He ties the decision to purchase equipment not to the finances of the organization as he's done in the past, but directly to the pride that the family feels about being part of the manufacturing community. He provides information about the cost of equipment in the context of the lifespan of the generations of the family and the work of the factory. He's created a case based on what is far more important to the family than dollars. He's made his case in terms of legacy.

After the presentation, to make sure that the decision is now reversed, Bob increases his social rapport by participating in some of the family activities, including a fishing trip. The company acquires the new equipment in large part because Bob has become more aware of social intelligence. He has realized that being professional was not the role that had power; \ by being a part of the family, he would have greater success and greater power. The story touches on judicious use of power, appropriate social interactions, and getting along well with others, which was as much a problem for Bob as stubbornness was to the family patriarch.

Let's take a look at social intelligence in communicating bad news to a team:

After the unexpected death of a team member, Carol must motivate the team to complete the project by its due date, even with crisis among members. The company client is an international company, expecting production of a national-level project and is really unconcerned with the details of their tragedy. Carol has several advantages in communicating needs in that she too is authentically experiencing grief, and her presence as a leader and a friend is clear.

Carol schedules a meeting to discuss who can contribute more during this time while respecting that some team members will be unable to fill responsibilities that they typically would have completed. This includes the deceased team member's cousin and also her best friend, both of whom work on the team. By facilitating with respect and allowing for grief rather than trying to shut it off, Carol allowed the team to decide who would step in to the lead and take on more responsibilities.

In the story, you can notice the elements of SPACE. Carol is aware of the situational stress of the deadline and aware of the paralysis among team members because of the emotional reactions to the sudden loss. Her clarity of communication in the setting establishes a respect for the team members' emotions allowing for flexibility in project engagement, but also communicates with clarity that the schedule will remain the same.

Social Intelligence Skills

There are many skills in social intelligence—some are more nuanced than others—but each of us can use, no matter what our setting for leadership, these four components of social intelligence in almost every single social setting:

- assertiveness
- the ability to shift perceptual positions
- nurturing social resilience
- increasing our frustration tolerance

As I mentioned in the last chapter, assertiveness is one of the skills that really crosses both social and emotional intelligence and probably other forms of intelligence as well. Dr. Jonice Webb has a written a blog post where she identifies five components of assertiveness:[34]

1. Knowing what you feel, even in the middle of a difficult situation

2. Trusting that your feelings and ideas are valid and worthy of expression

3. Managing your feelings and putting them into words

4. Understanding the other person or people involved, how they feel and why

5. Taking into account the situation and setting

In order to improve our social intelligence, I think one of the most important things we can do is increase our efficacy in the area of assertive communication. Over the years I've frequently recommended book to clients in counseling called *When I Say No, I Feel Guilty*. It's essentially a guide book for

---

34   s.v. "The Five Skills of Assertiveness."

training people in the skill of assertive communication. Well, a person can read a book about it and go through many different examples and practice sessions.

I think these five points are truly helpful. In every situation where there's a need for effective communication, ask yourself, "How do I feel? What are my emotions?" Pick adjectives that describe those things.

Two, ask yourself, "Wow, is it fair for me to feel that way? Is it healthy for me to feel this way?' Maybe you need to change your statement like we talked about in a previous chapter.

Three, if you trust that your feelings and ideas are valid and worthy of expression, then put them into words: "I need _____." "I feel _____." "I want _____." It's a simple statement. It's neither passive nor aggressive; it's just assertive.

Four, by getting out of ourselves and into the lives of others, we actually begin to understand how other people feel and why. And this is why I think in any leadership position, it's important for the leader to move from behind the desk to the front lines—not on a periodic basis, but on a regular basis.

Often one of the biggest issues between labor and management in any size company is labor believes that management simply doesn't understand what it's like to have to provide the service directly to customers in the time frame required. By moving from the ivory towers down to where the people are, we can understand how other people feel, developing empathy and turning that into leadership.

The next skill I want to talk about is moving to a second or third perceptual position. This is a very important element of social intelligence. Often in Neurolinguistic Programming we talk about three different perceptual positions. If you haven't heard of NLP perceptual positions, you might remember first, second, and third-person point-of-view from your high-school English class. It's the same idea.

The first perceptual position is "me as me". Now, if I'm experiencing crisis, if I'm trying to interact between, let's say, customers and suppliers and the phone is ringing and there's deadlines and there's email and all of these things sort of going on at the same time, it's very hard to look at the big picture. In fact, it becomes easy for me to use the aspect of self-awareness that we talked about being beneficial earlier in an unhealthy way that only focuses on my own experiences and fails to see my connectedness to others. First perceptual position is "me as me" in any given situation.

The second perceptual position is "me looking through your eyes." It is, as the old saying goes, the ability to "walk a mile in another person's moccasins," to "step into someone else's shoes." This is a very helpful position to take before a discussion or negotiation with someone who may oppose you.

The third perceptual position is sometimes discussed in therapy and this is "me outside of me." I can even be "me outside of me, watching me watch me." It all begins to sound a bit complex here following all of the me's in the story. But what it's really about this is about being able to perceive ourselves from various vantage points. And the reason why we would want to do that is because we can decrease the intensity of a crisis or emotions, or increase our ability to see globally a situation or experience.

I often work with executives to help them develop the skills of moving easily to third perceptual position. I often use a patter similar to this to direct this process:

Close your eyes for a minute and pay attention to yourself. Notice your breathing, your heart rate, notice what it feels like to breathe the air in and out, what it feels like to think to thoughts you're thinking right now. This is the first perceptual position. And this is where many people operate as they go about the tasks of the day. Really aware of what they need to be aware of in order to do the things that they need to do.

But it can become valuable to be an outsider observing yourself. It gives you a new vantage on situations. If things get difficult, it can actually move you emotionally from the proximity of any crisis to a place where you can observe without as much emotional enmeshment.

So as your eyes continue to remain closed, imagine there's another you over on the other side of the room, and it's watching you. Watching you sitting in the chair right now, reading this book, breathing in and breathing out. Ask yourself what this other you is seeing. Are they seeing your posture in a way that's healthy or unhealthy? Are they seeing you fully associating with your eyes closed or sitting with your eyes open? Are they seeing you from a new emotional perspective? Tired, fatigued, happy, sad, glad, scared, excited, or exuberant? When you imagine the you on the other side of the room seeing you, is it seeing more than just you? Is it able to see peripheral vision, around you, the place and the setting where you are right now? Is it getting a better picture of you and your connection to this moment, this experience? Now go ahead and open your eyes.

This is just a short example of one technique, for developing the skill in the acuity of moving into the third perceptual position.

The next element of social intelligence is nurturing social resilience. Whether it's a formal group like a team or peer group, or just an informal social setting, colleagues or a family working together—these other people are powerful influencers. Fear of how others perceive us, especially when we've experienced negative feedback in the past, can paralyze our ability to communicate in leadership. Often people get frustrated when others are frustrated, and people become depressed when others are depressed. And we often lose our own motivation when surrounded by the unmotivated. Social resiliency is the ability to use our internal ego strength to remain strong even when social experiences are unsupportive or fail to meet our expectations. Many leaders find that this is a trait they already possess; maybe it's something you even identified in the core characteristic on the NSRI.

There is a balance here. Sometimes negative feedback should be a warning to use that information to make a change we need to make, to become more adaptable or flexible, or even find a new way to communicate. But in many situations, the opposite is true. By remaining resilient to group think, we can lead when others don't. Resiliency is about staying in the present, neither being paralyzed by the past nor living in fear of the future. Healthy resilience comes from self knowledge and ego strength, along with an ability to be fully engaged at this moment, knowing that the future will care for itself.

Perhaps the single greatest strategy for resilience is to recognize that we can only live one moment at a time and to let go of anxiety about the future by staying in the present. Each breath actually represents each moment. And notice throughout this book, I have said, "Take a breath. Pay attention to the breath." A popular admonition to people during a time of stress, whether it's emotional or physical stresses, is just breathe. But although it sounds simple, "Just breathing, paying attention to the breath," is actually a great strategy for staying in the moment and increasing resiliency. By paying attention to the breath, we have a focal point to withdraw from intrusive thoughts of the future or fear of the future, and to just be here despite difficulties.

One of our biggest roadblocks to living in the moment, to being resilient, is that we tend to follow thoughts or fears when we have them. A lot of people also try to stop fears and thoughts, by saying, "Oh, that was a bad thought. I shouldn't have said that. That was a fearful thought. I need to let go of that.' But by thinking about not experiencing something, we actually cause ourselves to think about that something.

For example, right now, don't think about a yellow jeep. Wherever you are reading this book, you can think about whatever you want, but don't think about a yellow jeep. Just make sure you don't think about the yellow jeep. Even tell yourself, "I will not think about the yellow jeep," and think about something else. Now, of course, what is it that you are thinking? You are thinking of a yellow jeep.

Our thoughts are like that–whether they are fears, or whether they are stressors, or whether they are frustrations, anger, resentment, or anything else that may keep us from being an effective leader. And rather than trying to stop those thoughts, the idea here in resiliency training is to simply stop following those thoughts, to simply label that as a thought—to say, "that's a thought," and let it be a thought without having to follow it. This is also a hallmark of what is called "mindful living." It's a strategy for resilience that we're actually going to explore and develop in a full chapter later on in this book.

The fourth skill or aspect of social intelligence that's helpful is increasing your frustration tolerance level. Albert Ellis coined the term "low frustration tolerance," which I think applies directly to social intelligence. Frustration tolerance is the idea that we all have a certain level of frustration that we can tolerate before we start employing emergency coping strategies, paradoxical or self-defeating behavior such as yelling or avoidance. High frustration tolerance is a great thing in stressful situations.

Think about your own tolerance level for frustration; can it be improved? Do you find yourself easily restless, irritable or discontent, especially when others don't seem to be following your leadership?

First, be aware of it. Recognize that frustration is occurring on a scalable level. Frustration at Level 1, frustration at a Level 2, frustration at a Level 5, frustration at a Level 7, 8, 9, 10. I always have my clients in therapy scale their experiences, states, and emotions on a scale of 1 to 10. If you find yourself experiencing frustration, accept it at the level where it is without frustration determining your outcome.

Once again, breathing is one of the most useful things that we do. Breathing immediately brings oxygen to the blood supply. Something as simple as a deep breath can change your physiology. Physiology changes your mood. Thus, breathing can help you cope with frustration.

To increase your frustration tolerance, make a decision to rise above frustration. This does not mean that you are ignoring it or suppressing it, but rather engaging in the mindful practice of not following it. You don't have to try to make your frustration go away or stop; just see it as it is, where it is. Let frustration be frustration without you becoming frustration. Once again, one of our future chapters focusing on mindfulness will actually hone these skills of increasing your frustration tolerance level.

Both emotional intelligence and social intelligence are constructs that have been adopted by academic universities as well business and companies providing leadership training throughout the globe. As a therapist, I've certainly found these principles to be useful in my interactions with individuals one-on-one. And I hope that this chapter and the previous chapter have encouraged you to look at some of the resources that are included in our bibliography so that you can expand your awareness of emotional intelligence and social intelligence. Using these resources, you are already becoming the smartest person you can possibly become–in whatever way it is that you excel.

Chapter Seven:

Finding Your Calling

Just this past week I got a telephone call from a therapist friend of mine who works in a community mental health setting. He feels that this is something he was called to do, to serve the community and to help other people with the talents and the communication skills that he has. But he has a family with several children. He's married and living in a rural area, and he is not paid a high salary.

As a result of his inability to earn a salary that can take care of the needs of his family, he has begun to look for opportunities. He is currently enrolled in a business master's degree program. He called me because he feels as if he will be trading in his calling for simply a job.

Calling is something we all have to wrestle with, whether we're in the business realm or whether we're in private practice or whether we're doing any type of work in an educational setting, a community setting, a traditional corporate setting, or a government setting.

What is your calling? How have you been called to leadership? That is really an important question. In an earlier chapter, we saw that my hotel clerk friend recognized that she was called to leadership from the position where she held her job.

Hopefully you've already began to recognize that leadership is bigger than a vocational choice or an executive function; rather, it is transformational in your own life as well as the lives of those who are a part of your world. In this chapter, I'm going to focus specifically on calling as it relates to vocation while hopefully preserving the idea that we can be called to lead in many other arenas of life.

Without a doubt one of the biggest questions we face in life is "What am I going to do?' We know that you have a gift for leadership or you wouldn't already be this far into the book. We can really ask the question this way: "How can I use my gift of leadership and whom am I going to lead?' For some, especially those new to a career or those changing vocations, the question might often be asked, "How might I find a leadership opportunity?'

I've intentionally used the world calling in this chapter of this course and the reason why is it implies a perfect fit with vocation. The world calling implies that this is what you are supposed to do, to utilize all of your talents and resources to the fullest potential you possess. In fact, the word *vocation* comes from the Latin verb *vocare*, which literally means to call or speak. (Think of our word *vocal.*)

The word *calling* is often used in a religious context. For example, what is it that God has called you to do? But *calling* as a word choice to explore your own perfect fit for leadership abilities can be looked at apart from a strictly religious context. In fact, even from a religious perspective, calling is often misunderstood. In Genesis it's interesting to note that work was a sign before man's exile from the Garden of Eden (Genesis 2:15). This realization is pretty profound. It means that we were created to work, that work is not punishment, and that work has meaning and value. But people often think from a religious context or from their background with Judeo-Christian religion that work is punishment, and that calling refers to some sort of special work or benevolent work with a higher reward or a higher value.

Often the word *calling* is understood in a hierarchical context; people often believe that being called to a specific job is better than just getting a job. For example, "I was called to be a teacher," or "I was called to be a law enforcement officer," or "I was called to serve in the military." Those who subscribe to such a metaphysical concept of calling often view ecclesiastical work, nonprofit sector work, or government work as being special. This creates a dichotomy in which certain work is considered more important than the work regular people do such as sales, manufacturing, customer service, or running a cupcake shop or a pizza parlor.

I really want to challenge this notion that some work is more important than other work. The challenge can be both philosophical as well as pragmatic. From a philosophical plane, we're designed to carry out different kinds of work. Incredible meaning can be derived even from commercial endeavors. A couple of years back, I was in a classroom where an executive from Coca-Cola was sharing her story of finding her own joy at work as an executive for Coca-Cola. Several members of the class really began to smirk, saying, "How can there possibly be a higher calling in selling Coca-Cola? After all Coca-Cola is an unhealthy product."

Now recognize that these were people in a classroom in America, a country that right now is certainly concerned about what's healthy and what's unhealthy. We have an organic food movement versus foods which may have preservatives or additives. These really are some big issues for many different people. I'm not advocating unhealthy food, but many people from the vantage point simply looked at Coca-Cola as producing a product that is detrimental for a person.

I wholeheartedly agree that drinking a twelve-pack of Coke a day would be an unhealthy thing to do. In fact, in my own life I probably drink a Coca-Cola less than once a month, every now and then after I eat a big meal for some reason I like to have a half of a Coke. I'll even say to the waitress, "Please bring me a half a glass filled with Coke," and I have that as my dessert every once in a while when I'm out for dinner. But as I was listening to this Coca-Cola executive talk about finding meaning in her work and recognizing the disconnect that some of the students in that class were having because they recognized Coke as an unhealthy product, I thought of my own experiences in the Philippines.

A family I know in the Philippines was actually saved by Coca-Cola. The father in the family in the 1960s was given a license to bottle Coca-Cola. Having a license to bottle and sell Coca-Cola, the family certainly did very well and ended up becoming quite wealthy. But something really important happened in that community. Not only did the patriarch in that family acquire wealth by owning a bottling company, but people in that community who otherwise had been unemployed found work in his bottling plant during some very difficult time periods in the history of the Philippines.

In addition to that, while I certainly don't advocate Coca-Cola as the healthiest of all beverages, oddly enough it was healthier than the beer that Filipinos were drinking at the time. Why were they drinking beer? They were drinking that beer because the water sources they had were impure. Coca-Cola provided an alternative to intoxicants that was safe from bacteria and other contaminants that could put a person's life in jeopardy with diseases such as dysentery. This gave the local community an opportunity to have a beverage that in many cases probably preserved life in some degree or another. Our vantage point of what is good and what is bad really depends on the perceptual position where we are.

On a philosophical level our work might be the task that we complete every day—selling a car, delivering a pizza, delivering a sermon, counseling people—but ultimately the work that we choose to do represents our talents, our gifts and character, which is something almost every world religion that I'm aware of elevates over specific positions. On a pragmatic level it would be impossible for all of us to be nurses, clergy, counselors, teachers, or other helping professionals. Where would such people eat their lunch if there were no cafeteria workers or cash register manufacturers?

As a counselor I have an office where I see clients, and next door to my office is Qdoba Mexican Restaurant. I'm very grateful that people have decided to make serving high-quality Mexican food at the restaurant next door to my office their calling. The manager has been there as long as I've been going in there, which has probably been more than ten years. I'm grateful for him because without that nourishment to fuel my body I would be unable to meet the needs of the clients whom I work with in counseling and psychotherapy.

The point of all of this is that we're really called first to use our talents and gifts, but where we choose to use them is really an area with great flexibility. I believe that my friend who is in his MBA program will find that many of the talents and gifts that he uses as a therapist are things that he will be able to utilize in his work in business. He'll find that those same talents help him derive meaning from work in business just as they do in counseling. I don't know what he will do when he finishes his MBA, whether he will go into human resources or whether he will go into finance or some other area of business.

But I do know that therapists are trained in problem-solving. That's the talent and gift. Problem-solving can be applied with mentally ill clients in a community mental health setting. Likewise, it's useful with the clients I often see who are not mentally ill but are aspiring to make personal changes that are important to them. The ability to problem solve within a company which can have profound results for individuals. It can preserve employment. It can provide security to families. It can accomplish many objectives that really are highly beneficial for the community.

My friend from Chapter One, the hotel desk clerk, was using her gift of leadership as an ordinary hourly employee. As a counselor I meet many people who really struggle with the place or the specific position to where they are called. I think such a limited understanding of calling can create great emotional dissatisfaction and in many cases lead to depression, feelings of inferiority, or even feelings of doing the wrong thing. I'll share a personal example with you.

In my own life when I was a kid I was actually told that I was called to be a pastor. That's what the friends and family around me said. But I'm not a pastor. I'm a licensed counselor in private practice. In my own life I always felt like I would like to in an important big city, like New York, Los Angeles, or Chicago. Yet I've actually spent the last 25 years in Tulsa, Oklahoma, or Wichita, Kansas, both of which are nice but small cities. Neither of them are metropolitan centers of super importance.

For many years I struggled with the idea of calling. I wasn't in the big city, I wasn't the pastor. And I found freedom only when I realized that the title I held or the place where I practiced was of little importance compared to my ability to impact others and use my natural talents and gifts. I found freedom from a limited understanding of calling when I realized helping a cancer patient in Tulsa prepare for surgery by teaching mindfulness-based stress reduction was as important as being a pastor in Los Angeles and speaking to 5,000 people.

Probably the best known book addressing the subject of calling or answering the question of "What should I do?" is a book that's been released in multiple editions over the years, regularly updated, called *What Color is Your Parachute*. Richard Boles, the author of that book, really sums it up best when he says, "Always define what you want to do with your life and what you have to offer the world in terms of your favorite gifts, talents, skills, not in terms of a job title."[35]

I'm a believer that when we do our best, we find satisfaction no matter where we go. To begin to find your calling as a transformational leader, there are some steps that you can take.

One, embrace your strengths and resources, those things that you assessed in Chapter Three, and seek opportunity to draw from them in everyday situations.

Two, live fully in the present. Leadership begins right now, this very moment, not when you find a place. As you're reading this, take in a breath. Breathe in, breathe out, and recognize that at this moment you are fulfilling

---

35 Mark Emery Bolles, Richard Nelson Bolles, and Mark Bolles, *What Color Is Your Parachute?: Guide to Job-Hunting Online*, 6th ed. (Berkeley: Ten Speed Press, 2011).

the characteristics of a leader by preparing yourself in many different ways to not only assist others, but also to make significant change in the world while positively impacting other people.

Three, network with like-minded leaders. Go to lunch. Start an entrepreneur group in your area. Cold call exemplars and ask if you can meet with them. That's something that I've done. Just like a salesman who cold calls trying to prospect for a sale, you can cold call exemplars. Exemplars are those people who are in leadership positions or leaders whom you've seen successfully impact the community and even transform themselves. Ask if you can meet with them. Tell them the reason why is you're looking for somebody to mentor you, to teach you, or to simply learn from. Years ago I participated in a group of entrepreneurs where we could learn from each other. This turned out to be a great place to network not only for business leads and prospects, but also for leadership development skills.

Four, find out what other people call a problem and apply appreciative assessment to it. In other words, look at it from an entirely different perspective, seeing what's right rather than what's wrong. In our traditional model, for example, a company might be concerned that their customer complaint level is at 4%, so what they do is focus on the problem and try to figure out why are 4% of the people unhappy. The appreciative assessment model says, "Wow 96% of the people are happy. What have we been doing right and how can we do more of that?'

Five, volunteer to use your talents. This is a great way to find your calling, to get out of yourself and into the lives of other people. There are many places to volunteer your talents, ranging from religious organizations to government organizations to secular organizations. One friend of mine volunteers to teach meditation and self-management techniques at his local jail, for example.

Six, apply for positions rather than waiting for them to find you. This is something I think is really important. A lot of people believe because they've gotten online and gone to Monster.com or because they're on LinkedIn.com, people will start flooding them with opportunities for leadership positions. We need to use the networks that we create to actually apply for positions, to ask people for opportunities.

I did this just recently. I called one of those people from my entrepreneur networking group, who probably assumed that I would never be looking for a job because I have my own company doing my own thing. Although I currently am not looking for a job, I'm always looking for opportunities to use my talents with new markets and to have new experiences and opportunities.

So I called him up and said, "Hey can we go eat lunch?" And he said "Sure." When I went to lunch I brought my résumé with me and I told him I was here to apply for a job, not a fulltime job, not a job working the office, but a job fulfilling a specific niche that I knew that he needed to utilize some of the talents that I had. He was surprised, but he gave me an opportunity.

Seven, give yourself permission to change your mind. This is something that's really important. So many people believe that changing their mind is something just awful. They think it means that a person doesn't have stick-to-itiveness or discipline or any other number of superlatives to define not doing so well.

The reality is that nothing lasts forever. I had a friend who used to say, "It's all going to burn in the end anyway." It didn't sound real positive, but it actually was. It was freeing a person from the idea that they can't change their mind.

Eight, seek out every opportunity that you have for personal growth: to take a class, to gain new perspectives, to have different and unique personal interactions. All of these things can help you to fulfill your calling.

Calling is actually such a fundamental part of Transformational Leadership that Bass and Riggio traced the history of Burns' work and noted that early on it was apparent that Transformational Leadership was not dependent on position or title.[36] They observed that it should extend throughout organizational hierarchy from those we view as being at the top, the CEO, to those we view as being at the bottom, the person who cleans the latrines. They write:

> It becomes clear that every member on a team could learn to be transformational. It's not routine to talk about Transformational Leadership at the shared team level. What this confirms is that the ability to transformational is not dependent on a specific calling but rather a broader understanding that we can be called to leadership from any position.

In a previous chapter, I stressed that leadership is not something to aspire to, but something to discover. To use Tony Robbins' metaphor, it is "something that we can unleash from within." I stressed that you already possess within you that which will guide you through your calling to emergence as a

---

36   Bass and Riggio. 185.

leader and that the strengths unique to you are the starting point for fulfilling this calling as a leader.

Many people I speak with still don't feel capable or ready to lead. There is something holding back from fulfilling this calling that goes beyond a limiting belief about what calling is. And these things that are holding us back are often our drives. Rick Warren in his book *The Purpose Driven Life* tells us that "everybody's life is driven by something."[37]

Unfortunately, Warren's observations as a pastor are the same as my observations as a therapist. He tells us that there are five common drives which are really holding us back. I've seen these in my therapeutic practice as well—people who are driven by guilt, driven by resentment and anger, driven by fear, driven by materialism, or driven by the need for approval.

The alternative to being driven by any of these is to be driven by purpose, which is, of course, far different than being driven by position or title. To do this, go back to the strengths you identified in Chapter Three and begin looking each day for a way to apply those strengths with intentionality. Intentionality is a concept that's rarely discussed, but it's probably one which could actually fill its own course. Intentionality is goal-directed and purposeful behavior. Intentionality is mindful. Intentionality is about something—in our case, it's about transformation.

Let me share with you a great example of intentionality. Joseph Asym went from being a baggage handler to the CEO of a multimillion dollar marketing and design company that generates over $350 million a year in sales.[38] He grew up poor but in a wealthy area. With intention, he not only set goals, but he did the work to achieve them.

He says in a YouTube video that he was inspired to work by seeing his parents struggle working three jobs just to get him through Concordia University. He says that people say, "You're lucky," when they see his success, but he answers, "Luck has nothing to do with it. It was intentionality, perseverance." He says, "Without ambition, one starts nothing. Without work, one finishes nothing."

The task of the transformational leader is really twofold. First they define their own calling according to their God-given talents and strengths to create

37   Richard Warren, *The Purpose Driven Life: What on Earth Am I Here For?*, Expanded ed. (Grand Rapids, Mich.: Zondervan, 2012).

38   PracticeWhatUWant, 2013. "From Struggle Comes Success -- Inspirational Video," From Struggle Comes Success -- Inspirational Video. http://youtu.be/ObD0F0vJSJA

a purpose-driven life. Second, the transformational leader is willing to guide and mentor others through that same process.

We're going to talk more about mentoring in our next chapter, but I want to share with you how I actually became a therapist rather than a pastor. Part of it had to with the leaders who were in my life at that time. One of those leaders was particularly transformational, and the other leader wasn't.

After I finished my Bachelor's Degree in Ministry, I took my first job as the associate pastor or youth pastor of a small church. It was interesting. The pastor was very much focused on himself, so he wasn't particularly focused on helping me develop in my role. He wanted to make sure I was busy and that I had lessons prepared each Sunday morning. But beyond holding me accountable for the job description of youth pastor, he really didn't pay too much personal attention to me.

About that same time I took a second job as a psychiatric technician in a therapy setting where the executive director of this organization would bring me into the office and regularly ask for my opinion and my feedback. He wanted to hear the observations that I was making on the floor working with patients eight hours a day. It seemed kind of amazing to me that the executive director would be interested in what I had to say especially since I was new and really didn't have much experience.

His style of leadership, which included mentorship as an important component, helped me to make the decision as to which path I would eventually follow. The result was that I chose a valued path as a psychotherapist, as a counselor. Either position actually would have been fine. My calling wasn't to a particular job. My calling was to using my talents and skills to help other people. Now, I answer that calling mostly in the role of a teacher working with a wide variety of students who then go on to impact many people in positive ways.

Chapter Eight:

Mentorship

As you recall from Chapter One, the fifth and final aspect in Randy Dobbs' model of Transformational Leadership is of course leaving behind a cadre of future transformational leaders.

There is really only one way of effectively doing that: mentorship. One of my favorite proverbs has always been the proverb that says "As irons sharpens iron, so one man sharpens another." (Proverbs 27:17)

Now of course if this were written in the year 2015, it would say, "As iron sharpens iron, so one person sharpens another." I just want to point that out because men can mentor men, and women can mentor women, and women can mentor men, and men can effectively mentor women. Leadership is not for any specific gender but should be available of course to all people.

Dobbs tell us that the most lasting mark for any leader will be that the transformation does not stop.[39] Effective Transformational Leadership is like a perpetual motion machine. It's not dependent on one person. It is sustainable within a community or organization, and it becomes part of a larger culture of transformation as well as a culture of leadership.

Mentorship is really the key to building this perpetual motion machine. Without mentorship, leading really is just changework. It's temporary. It fails to become self-sustaining and often dies with the originator. This is actually the problem with certain charismatic leaders. The change is temporary because the leadership and the change often die with the originator. The mistake of too many charismatic leaders is to let a great work die out without a plan for succession. They never transform others to do the work of a leader.

---

39   Dobbs.

Sometimes this error is made because a young leader believes that there is time to develop a legacy later. But of course the future is unknown, and for that reason Transformational Leadership is a leadership which begins finding partners, additional leaders, and training others from the very outset.

In therapy I learned that discharge-planning actually begins in the very first session. This is the same concept that really is true in any discipline where we are functioning as a leader. We often ask the question in the very first session of therapy, "What's the plan when therapy is done? Whom can this client connect with? What resources do they have available to them? Where can they go and how can they function autonomously and independently?" Ideally the goal of good psychotherapy is for the client not to have to come back anymore.

In fact, I always tell therapists you know you're a good therapist when your clients no longer need you. This principle is true in really every aspect of leadership from business to government to community development and even in ministry settings. As you move into a leadership role, you must ask yourself these questions:

With whom can I partner?
Whom can I mentor so that I have other leaders leading with me?

These questions help the transformational leader share workloads and responsibilities, but more importantly, they help create a larger foundation for organizational and interpersonal success.

Now let's talk for a moment about where the word *mentor* came from. It's really a pretty interesting story. It is of course from Greek mythology; Mentor is a character in Homer's *Odyssey*. In the story, Odysseus is fighting in the Trojan War and he trusts his son Telemachus to Mentor, who becomes the overseer of Telemachus. The Goddess Athena goes to visit Telemachus and takes the disguise of Mentor to hide herself from the suitors of his mother. This was viewed as a pragmatic and practical plan for dealing with personal dilemma.

The result, of course, is that we have the concept of a mentor, a wise teacher who invests in the success and wellbeing of those that he is charged with overseeing. In the 1699 book, *The Adventures of Telemachus,* by Fenelon, the tutor Mentor gives advice, and teaches others how to lead by giving speeches and advice. One of the key elements of Mentor in this book is the pragmatic approach to life, which emphasizes altruism over consumption and luxury. He is also an advocate for participatory government.

From these two sources, the word *mentor* has come into our popular vo-cabulary. There are so many elements of these two writings that characterize what we now recognize as mentorship. Both the original story of Homer, as well as the further work of Fenelon, share with us these characteristics of a mentor: care, wisdom, community, teaching, advice, pragmatism, responsi-bility, training.

In his chapter on nurturing potential leaders in the book *Developing Leaders Around You*, John Maxwell stresses that many organizations fail to tap into their potential because they are in a transactional model, exchanging a paycheck for a task. Maxwell tells us, "Successful organizations take a different approach. In exchange for the work a person gives he receives not only his paycheck but a nurturing from the people for whom he works."[40]

This nurturing is in fact mentorship. That's what Maxwell is talking about. Maxwell suggests a strategy for building others into leaders, and he gives us the acronym BEST for that strategy:

- Believe in them

- Encourage them

- Share with them

- Trust them

Now for those who are in positions of authority and responsibility, such as a CEO or department manager, it is sometimes easy to see people who are below that level of responsibility as lacking adequate skills, appropriate per-sonality traits, natural inclinations, or abilities to solve problems on their own.

But leadership is about mentoring people so that they can develop these things. The effective transformational leader recognizes that while skill devel-opment can be a part of leadership training, believing in your people from the very beginning is important.

Encouraging them will do two things: It will help you to step into your belief in their capacity to lead, and it will help them step into the confidence necessary to succeed.

By sharing our knowledge, our skills, and our time, we give our people the tools to be able to experience success.

---

40   John C. Maxwell, *Developing the Leaders around You* (Nashville, Tenn.: T. Nelson, 1995).

Finally, trust is important. Trust is actually a reflection of ourselves and the knowledge that we've taken the time to do our best with individuals. By trusting them, we actually trust ourselves.

Let me share with you two negative experiences that I had relating to mentorship. I've had many positive experiences in life, and part of this chapter will include a short interview with Alex Nongard about his positive experiences with mentorship. But first I'm going to share with you two experiences that I had.

The first one was the oddest experience that I've ever had in what I would have believed or perceived should be a mentoring relationship, and that was one of my first jobs.

In the previous chapter, I wrote about my experience as a youth pastor at a church. I was really excited about the opportunity to move into this role. I had interviewed with the church's board of directors, the pastor, and the families of the youth—and I got along great with all of them. This job seemed to be a wonderful opportunity. It was a part-time, twenty-hour-a-week position that I hoped would eventually grow into a full-time a career as an associate pastor.

However, something interesting happened. The very first day of my job I brought over some of the books from my library, and I put them in my new office. I cleaned up the desk that was there, added some decorations to the wall, and the sat in my new office, excited about the opportunity which I had to impact families in the church.

The pastor, that very first day, poked his head in the door. He said, "Hello, great to have you here," and then he moved off to his office. I'm assuming being the senior pastor and not having an associate at this point, he had a lot of work to do, which is of course understandable. I began to talk to some of the people who were around that building that day—the maintenance guy at the facilities, the church secretary, some of the families who came in—simply introducing myself and saying hello to those I didn't know. I spent the day asking questions about their families, about their experiences at the church, and about the history of the town where I was. It was really an awesome first day.

On the second day, I showed up and sat in my office for a few minutes. Some of the other staff members showed up, including the pastor who waved as he walked by my door and went off to his office. I thought it was a little odd that the pastor really hadn't come into my office or invited me into his office. The second day I would have imagined he would begin the process of mentoring, of not only praying with me, but also of teaching me some of the things and sharing his vision with me, which is something that occurred at least to some extent during the interview process.

Day three I showed up, and the same thing happened again. Now I was thinking it was really strange. It was really odd. I sat back in my chair, and I thought to myself "Why was I hired? What is the vision?' The pastor expressed that it was important to hire me in the interview process and in the conversations that we'd had up to that point. But now that I was here he seemed rather uninterested in my presence.

A week went by, two weeks went by, and the senior pastor had never called me into his office. He had never come into my office. He had never scheduled a time for us to pray, a time for us to talk about the vision, a time for us to really connect about the families within the church. Again, I found this to be truly odd. I went into his office. I knocked on the door. I said "Hey it's great to be here. I've really enjoyed the last couple of weeks and meeting with and working with the families. Let's have a little conversation about your vision and some of the things that I can do to support your ministry."

He said, "Sure, come on in and have a seat," but he seemed uninterested in me being there. He talked a little bit about the importance of what it is that I would be doing and some of the things within the denomination that were of concern to him. But he really seemed to be uninterested again in my presence. I left that meeting really confused.

Other the next couple of months, it became apparent to me that I was not hired for any reason other than I had standing with the denomination. That was the only reason that I was hired. What that means is that I was eligible to vote at the regional meeting both on behalf of the church as well on behalf of myself. And I discovered that the pastor did not have standing with the denomination.

This was something that wasn't made known to me before I accepted the position. It was information that was withheld. It turns out that I was actually hired for one reason and one reason only, and that was because of denominational politics and the pastor's refusal to become ordained by the denomination, choosing instead to be ordained only by the church. It was a complex and strange scenario. Obviously, it didn't last very long. It didn't turn into a career. I stayed there for probably about six to eight months, and I enjoyed working with some of the families and hopefully impacting some of the kids in a positive way in the short time I was there.

I remember recognizing that mentoring was not on the table and investment in my position was not something that was on the table, so I turned in my resignation, leaving that position as the youth pastor.

I share that story with you because it was something that affected me for many years. It was something that in the short-term resulted in depression. It was something that in the short-term resulted in a feeling of disappointment. It was something that in the short run really left me sad. But this situation was important to me because it helped me to recognize the importance of truly investing in those whom I have a responsibility to mentor, guide, and lead.

Even though it wasn't a good situation for me, it probably was a good situation for those whom I have supervised in various positions since that point because I've made an effort right off the bat to let those people I work with know that I feel that their presence is important, that I believe in them, that I want to encourage them, that I have something to share with them, and that I will, in fact, trust them.

I had another learning experience years later. I was hired to manage a specific project because of specialized skills that I had. But again, the same thing occurred: the CEO was uninterested in spending time with me. The CEO did not invest in sharing with me. I was given no authority beyond the immediate project. I finished the project successfully, and people were happy with my work. It really was an experience that harkened back to the days of that very first experience as a youth pastor where mentorship was clearly not present.

I've shared with you two negative experiences, but I've had plenty of positive experiences with mentors who took the time to believe in me, encourage me, share with me, and trust me. As a matter of fact, I had a boss many years ago. When my two oldest kids were born, I worked for a guy named Richard Foresee. Not only was he a terrific mentor in my position as a therapist, but he had raised five daughters as a single parent.

I myself grew up in a family where there was divorce. My father died when I was young. There was some conflict with my stepbrother, stepsisters, and stepfather after my mother remarried. It was a little on the chaotic side. When my children were born, I really didn't know how to parent. I remember saying to Richard, who had mentored me on many issues related to work, "Hey I know that you have five daughters that you've raised, how do you parent?' Not only did he mentor me in my professional career, but he mentored me as a parent as well.

I had another excellent mentor in my early years as well. I'll call him out, too; his name is JT Darpino. He has been a leader in substance abuse treatment services for almost three decades. He taught me about business. He taught me about therapy. He taught me about interacting in a corporate environment. He spent time with me. He took me to lunch. He believed in me, encouraged me, shared with me and trusted me. JT mentored me by building rapport, giving me autonomy under supervision and having my back when things got tough.

As a result of these and other positive mentoring experiences I've had, I've observed that there are four strategies for effective mentorship at the heart of realizing your full potential as a transformational leader. They are essentially a pathway to creating a cadre of leaders to leave behind when you are done.

The first strategy is to invest your time.

Sometimes in therapy parents say to me, "It's not the quantity of time I spend with my children. It's the quality of time." And I always let them know that they're wrong—that it actually is the quantity. The message a child gets when a parent does not spend time with them is, "You are worth less than my time."

If you don't have time to mentor, you really don't have time to lead. You must spend time with those who you are leading and mentoring. When you do not spend time with someone you are supposed to believe in, you're really sending a message that is incongruent with the belief. Investing time means attending to somebody. It means being present. It means not only going to lunch, but simply sitting and being present with somebody perhaps while they're working on something else.

There have been many times when a mentor I was working with had something to do that was important, and I had something to do that was different, but we sat at a coffee shop with laptops across from each other, each doing our work independently, simply being with one another.

The second strategy for effective mentorship is to utilize the positive strengths.

This is really the heart of action-oriented encouragement. Approach mentorees with positive psychology and appreciative inquiry, drawing on what they have done right rather than being disappointed by their deficits.

Whenever I work with couples in marriage counseling, I can't fix what's wrong with them. I don't have time, and there are usually too many things that are wrong. Instead, what I do is take that which is right and help them to strengthen it. I give all the couples I work with the same assignment:

> *On the way home from this first session, stop and buy a spiral notebook. Write down the "Smith Family Treasure Chest" on the front. (Obviously, substitute your own name for "Smith!") I call this assignment "one book, two people." It doesn't matter if you do this together, if you talk about this, or if you don't talk about it. Just take the book and put it in a room—the bedroom, the bathroom, the garage, the kitchen—it doesn't matter where it is, as long as each of you pass through each day. Write down one thing you value about your partner each day, one word, one sentence, one short paragraph.*

For most couples this is the first time they've focused on what's right with their partner rather than what's wrong with their partner in many, many years. Doing this treasure chest assignment changes the entire dynamics of that relationship. It is a homework assignment based on positive psychology or appreciative inquiry. And it's amazing how I can take what's right with the couple and use that to strengthen the relationship and have a greater level of efficacy than if I try to fix what's wrong with them.

The third hallmark or third element of effective mentorship is to share everything,

especially credit as a leader. I did have one other negative experience with mentorship and that was very early on. I had actually written a paper or a proposal for an inpatient psychiatric unit where I worked. I had outlined a protocol for working with clients that I thought would be highly effective. We began to implement that protocol.

The manager of that department was an academic who regularly wrote journal articles. What is interesting is that as I was reading one of the journals about a year after the program was implemented I found an article that she had written in a publication that really described exactly what I had proposed and what I was doing. Essentially she had taken credit in an academic journal for my work with no mention of my role, my position, or my name. She had not even asked me in any way if my idea could be shared. It's important to share resources, to share your mentor with your mentorees, to share your emotions, to share the financial rewards of success.

It's interesting in the field of restaurant management and restaurant training a new waiter or waitress usually has to follow somebody more experienced for a few days. As a new waiter or waitress follows somebody for a few days, they are usually assigned some of their own tables by the head waiter whom they're following. But the head waiter gets all of the tips because the waiter who is in training is of course getting a fulltime rate equal to minimum wage. And some of the waiters who train other waiters take all of those tips, yet some of them—usually the better waiters, by the way—share those financial rewards with those they are training, not out of obligation, but because they recognize that it's important. They realize that in doing so they can create for themselves more effective relationships and teams that will serve them over the next year or two.

The fourth method or strategy is to ask questions.

Use questions from positive psychology and positive inquiry to draw on the strengths and push your mentorees into the next level.

Perhaps the most important aspect of being an effective mentor is to get your own mentor. No one is beyond benefiting from mentorship. Take initiative. Ask someone to specifically mentor you. I meet therapists who work without clinical supervisors and CEOs who don't have any accountability except the board. Usually they have not developed those personal mentor/mentee relationships that could benefit them and help them to grow in their role as a CEO. I think getting your own mentor and being a mentee is probably one of the most effective ways to be an effective mentor and leave behind a cadre of future transformational leaders.

Chapter Nine:

Leadership Communication

This chapter is titled "Leadership Communication," or as I like to call it, "The Sudoku of Communication." I think of these specific strategies for communication as adding up on every level to irrefutably positive success.

Communication strategies are the basis for all human interaction; communication is the basis of effective hierarchical functioning as well as lateral relationships across departments, families, or communities. It's how a large company engages customers and sets itself apart from competition. Communication defines a Board and CEO's relationship, and it defines the effectiveness of advertising, personnel management, team functioning, and almost every aspect of any for-profit and non-profit organization.

Although I've yet to meet anyone to dispute the importance of effective communication, I do meet a lot of leaders, employees, and managers who've failed, at even the most basic level, to use communication to create success.

Effective communication is:

- How a leader shares a vision, and more importantly, has that vision adopted by the team as their own vision.

- How relationships are built cross-culturally, in ways that lead to increased sales, improved team functioning, and a decrease of stress.

- The heart of mentoring and developing the full potential of others–one of the hallmarks of transformational leadership.

- How deals are closed. It's how value is built and how problems are solved.

Let's talk for a minute about Sudoku, a wildly popular game played by millions of people. Every time I go to an airport, a coffee shop, or a waiting room, I look around and see other people playing this game. You've probably seen it also. It's really a simple game. Although it can be played electronically on a tablet or phone, it's usually played with just a pencil and a piece of paper–kind of like tic-tac-toe or crossword puzzles. It's remarkably simple, yet paradoxically complex.

Because I've seen so many people play in so many places, I bought a Sudoku and learned how to play. I have to admit I'm neither a skilled nor an avid player. I've probably played no more than a handful of Sudoku games in my life, although I have enjoyed it. I'm not an expert, just a casual player.

What I've learned about Sudoku is that the game makes a great metaphor for successful communication. First, Sudoku is a logic game, not a math game. It's played on a grid of nine boxes, with some numbers filled in to start and others left blank. The object is simple. The player has to use logic to determine which number is missing from each square; the key is that each row in each of the nine 3x3 sub-grids that compose the grid, which are called "boxes," has to contain all of the digits from one to nine. There's only one solution to each puzzle, and all of the columns and all of the boxes will add up to a single number in each box, with no numbers replicated. Because Sudoku is composed of nine boxes within a game of nine grids, it can be pretty difficult to make sure that not only each box, but each of the larger columns and rows, adds up to a unique single digit.

This is where our metaphor between the game of Sudoku and Effective Communication begins.

First, effective communication is logical. Formulas for effective communication yield predictable results. At any level of an organization, across departments, and even to customers, the communication must add up to a unified message. If not, mistakes are made, and problems occur.

For example, suppose the center box represents the marketing department, which makes a decision about a promotion, but the communication doesn't add up. The finance department can become quite upset about temporary changes to the revenue, and the customer service department might actually be exacerbating this by inadvertently doubling the promotion by giving 10% off rather than $10 off.

This mistake might not be caught until it's been replicated throughout the system, eventually crashing the expected results of the CEO or the Board.

In the end, the customers might even be asked to forgo the promotion they were awarded as the offer is corrected, which means customer service might experience a spike in complaints or customer dissatisfaction.

Communication—it must add up on every level or the results can be disastrous for any organization.

The same metaphor works in family communication, whether that's communication between the parent and child, parent to parent, child to friend, family to family in the school or neighborhood, or even among extended family members. When the communication does not add up on every level, it can have disastrous consequences.

To win at Sudoku, one must have a strategy. The basic strategy is to solve the puzzle. Players work on every Sudoku game from the easy ones to the most difficult ones. Similarly, to avoid disastering communication we need a strategy.

Strategies of Effective Communication

There are nine strategies of effective communication that have irrefutable outcomes. They always add up to a predictable result.

Strategy 1: Proxemics

Have you ever had someone who was a close talker invade your personal space and just start talking to you? Have you ever had a stranger sit next to you in a public place, where there were other places that person could have chosen that weren't so close? Have you ever been in another country or culture where the rules of personal space and conversation, which you have become accustomed to, were different? Do you ever feel like all of the texting, e-mailing, and online communication that we engage in are contributing to an inability of people to engage in appropriate conversation?

In a New York Times article, Stephanie Rosenbloom writes, "Communications scholars began studying personal space and people's perception of it decades ago in a field known as proxemics. With the population of the United States climbing above 300 million, urban corridors becoming denser and people with wealth searching for new ways to separate themselves from the masses, interest in the issue of personal space—that invisible force field around your bod—is intensified."[41]

Proxemics is an important aspect of communication. Researchers have found that when customers are looking at a store, contemplating whether or not to enter, if they're brushed against by another customer, they will often choose to simply walk away and not enter the store.

The science of proxemics is important. It can tell an architect how wide to make corridors so that people don't bump into each other. It tells those setting up racks or displays in merchandising how far apart to put those things, so that shoppers can feel like they have intimacy within their personal space without being intruded upon by others, which could increase their discomfort level and chase them from a store.

Edward Hall is the anthropologist who is considered the "Father of Proxemics." He actually outlined measurements of what personal space is considered in the U.S.A. He defines these numbers:

Intimate distance: 6 – 18 inches

Personal distance: 18 inches – 4 feet

Social distance: 4 feet – 12 feet

Public distance: 12 feet or more

Within each of those personal space bubbles, there is an appropriate way to interact with other people. Now of course, displays and corridors are not going to be 12 feet apart. You will have people intruding your personal and intimate space in public settings. The unwritten rule is that as long as they are moving along and preferably not making eye contact, rather than stopping in your personal space, such passage is permitted.

Every culture has unwritten rules about the correct use of personal space. What's interesting is that these rules we have about personal space even extend to functionalized versions of reality. Players of the game Second Life–which is an online game where people use avatars in an anonymous online environment–continued to utilize these same rules, even in online play.

Violating unwritten rules of personal space can be interpreted as aggressive, dishonest, sexual, insulting, or disrespectful. In the business or

---

41　　Stephanie Rosenbloom, The New York Times http://www.nytimes.com/2006/11/16/fashion/16space.html?8dpc=&_r=2&oref=slogin&pagewanted=print& (accessed March 8 2014).

community environment, violating those rules can lead to difficulty in leadership status, failure to sell, or failure to close the deal, or even in the most extreme situations, lawsuits based on the appearance of impropriety.

There is a balance here, and at times it can be appropriate or even good for the rules to be suspended. We just need to know when to suspend those rules. For example, when presenting to a large audience, a musician or a speaker might leave the stage and come down to the first couple of rows of the audience, and speak to them in a more personal space or distance.

This works, of course, because the first rows of an audience are connected to the back rows. It really communicates a non-verbal message: "I am with you; I'm attending to you."

Not too long ago, I went to see The Blue Man Group in Las Vegas, and one of the things that they did was leave the stage. They certainly entered into the social distance, as well as the personal distance of audience members, even the intimate distance of some of those audience members. When they did that, they created a sense of discomfort among those individuals, eventually breaking that discomfort by tapping them with special recognition to be a participant in the show.

People in the audience applauded and were happy for two reasons: one, they weren't hoisted on stage themselves, and two, they were glad that somebody from the regular crowd had a chance to be on stage and become a part of the show.

In fact, I think the Blue Man Group is one of the best shows in Las Vegas, and I've seen almost every single big show in Las Vegas. Part of the reason why is that the Blue Man Group performers have been able to utilize proxemics to create a sense of rapport with the audience by effectively breaking some of these rules of personal space.

I was at a lecture with my son. The speaker was the former Governor of Oklahoma, who's also a former Senator of Oklahoma, David Boren. In the 1990s he was certainly a national political figure. In fact several different people from several different parties had even considered David Boren as the Vice Presidential candidate, or perhaps had even encouraged him to run for President. He currently serves as the President of the University of Oklahoma.

My son and I went to hear him speak. Here's a person who has, on a global level, achieved status, accomplishment, notoriety, and leadership. His speech was empowering and impressive. When the speech was over, Dr. Boren left the stage and came out into the audience. The event was over, but he mingled with the guests. My son, who is going to be going to the University of Oklahoma next year, had a chance to take a picture with Dr. Boren, and I had a chance to say hello and talk to him for a few minutes.

By leaving the stage at the end of the event and entering the personal space of those who had been to his lecture, the excellent speaker endeared many people in the audience to him, inspiring them to support the work that he's currently doing as the President of the University of Oklahoma.

Strategy 2 – Eliciting a Transderivational Search

I think that this is one of the most powerful things that we can do to increase the success of our communication. A Transderivational Search– I often abbreviate it T.D.S.–causes a listener to look inside of them self, often for an answer or a response.

Are you ready to improve your communication level?

As soon as I ask that question, instead of focusing on me giving this lecture, you have to look inside of yourself to answer the question. By asking questions, and by creating a transderivational search, we can take a topic or a subject and really make it much more personal.

Let me give you two examples of a transderivational search:

Several years ago I was in Oklahoma at a downtown convenience store, and there was a homeless person out front. He had a sign that read "Will Work for Food." Folks carrying that sign are not an uncommon site in the downtown area. I parked my car, and I went in to the convenience store, stepping over his extended legs, which were jutting out into the sidewalk in front of the store, and I actually ignored him–just like 99.9% of the other people did.

I walked back out of the store, stepped back over his legs again in order to get to my car, got in my car, and started the car. That's when I looked up and saw him sitting on the sidewalk holding that sign that read, "Will Work for Food," just like everybody else's sign. I decided then to give him something better than my spare change.

I knew I had some cardboard in the back of my car, and I always carry Sharpies with me since I'm often teaching and doing lectures. So I turned the car off, went to the back of the car, and got out the cardboard; I grabbed a Sharpie, and I wrote a new sign. Then, I walked up to him and said, "Hey, here's five bucks. I'm an expert in NLP and psychology and communication, and I have a sign that I'm going to give you, which you can use if you'd like to, that I think would be a lot more effective for you."

He said, "Well what do you mean? What's wrong with my sign?"

I said, "Well, your sign is the same sign as everyone else's sign, and when I see you sign 'Will Work for Food,' it doesn't cause me to look inside of myself. I see you probably not working for food when you're holding that sign."

He looked at me with a lot of distrust and maybe even a little bit of hostility, and I flipped my sign over, and he looked at it. A big smile came across his face. My sign read, "What would you need if you were hungry?"

I had already given him the five bucks. I gave him the sign, and I said to him, "If you use this sign, I think you will double your income before the day is over."

The reason why is simple. Now when people see the sign, instead of seeing you, they have to see themselves; they have to answer the question, "What would I need if I were homeless?"

The transderivational search is a very powerful tool in communication to create an emotional response to a vision, a product, a suggestion, or anything else that we might be using, in either business or the community, to create success.

Earlier today I was showing a friend of my how e-Lance works. E-Lance is a website where people can post jobs and find people to do those jobs–often tech jobs. I've been using e-Lance for many years to find people ranging from programmers to graphic designers to transcriptionists. I use them on a regular basis. I've never actually bid on a job, but because I was showing a friend how to use e-Lance and how he could earn some money by bidding on jobs, I actually went through the process of bidding on a job.

There was a job posted, and it was to write advertising copy for a thirty-second and a sixty-second radio ad. Now, my profile as an employee or a consultant has 0 feedback, 0 jobs; I didn't even post my picture. I was simply bidding on the job to show him how it worked.

I got a reply back the next morning that said, "You've intrigued me, please tell me more. Can you send me a sample of your work?" So, I actually sent some radio ads that I had made for one of my businesses. How did I get the interest of that person? There were over twenty other people who had bid on the job, but he responded to my ad even though he should have ignored it. With no feedback, no picture, no prior history of doing any jobs on e-Lance, I should have been ignored.

The way that I got a response was I didn't start out focusing on me. I started out by focusing on the person who placed the ad. I stated at the beginning of my bid, "Would you like to have the confidence to know that your ad will be a success?" Then I went in to a short description of who I am, what I do, and how, by hiring me, they could achieve their goals. Again, I started my response, not by focusing on me, but by focusing on the listener instead. That's the transderivational search.

Strategy 3 – Storytelling

Storytelling is important. I just told you two stories. People enjoy stories; it's a way to connect others. When I tell you a story about something I did, you are probably thinking about something that you did.

Stories, metaphors, and parables are great tools in leadership. They shift filters of perception. For the listener, there's an unconscious meaning that bypasses any conscious resistance. For example, if I'm telling you something controversial or even something that you probably would disagree with, but I do it in the form of a story, there's not the level of resistance to hearing the story that you might have to my direct suggestion or even my command. So, a story can also serve to conceal a confrontation.

Over the years I've had employees whom I've had to confront, and I've often confronted them by telling them a story. It's decreased tension during that confrontation, and yet it communicated the same powerful truth. Storytelling is a powerful tool in communication because it's really an act of magical creation; it's a great way to share a vision, to get buy-in for an idea.

The storyteller has historically been the transmitter of cultural wisdom, and so when I tell stories, people look for the wisdom here. This goes back to Aesop's Fables and other stories of stature that have endured over time. Stories have a pervasive cultural and inter-generational life, and so as a tool for impacting people whose cultural experiences may be different than mine, storytelling can really facilitate an awareness of cross-cultural communication.

Strategy 4 – Knowing the Language Patterns that Produce Response

Now, I shared with you the transderivational search a few minutes ago, but there are many other effective language patterns.

Milton Erickson was a psychiatrist in the 1950s who was also a family therapist. There is a protocol that has been developed by studying Milton

Erickson, who was famously effective at helping people to make change, called The Milton Model. The idea is to use language patterns to capture a person's point of attention and then to create an internal experience or dialogue with the unconscious resources that they possess.

The purpose of the Milton Model is really to invite a person to respond, either internally and experientially, or verbally and behaviorally. You can see how useful this might be in leadership, in sales, in community development, or even in dealing with teenagers.

The Milton Model is known for using artfully vague language patterns to avoid a conscious objection by the participant or the imposition of my bias into the process of communication. These are really the core foundations of persuasion techniques, ranging from sales closing to a call to action or sharing a vision, or even getting donors to donate to a non-profit organization, or business leaders to support a community charitable cause.

Communication really is, to some extent, a form of manipulation–as are most human interactions. We're trying to get other people to adopt our ideas as their own ideas. This is why the Milton Model of communication can be an effective strategy in transformational leadership. This is also why leadership ethics are important. Milton Model techniques can be powerfully helpful or harmful, depending on the operator and the ego strength levels of the client.

In general, the Milton Model advocates avoiding specificity, because the more specific we are, the more likely there is to be opposition rather than rapport. For example, a speaker might use a sentence like this: "Can you imagine what success might be like? Each of us with our pressed and clean work uniforms, all standing near the red line in the warehouse now that sales have increased by 24% this quarter."

Now, that's an example of very specific language. I'm asking a person to essentially visualize where they're standing and what they're wearing, and I've attached a very specific number to the sales increase. A person listening to that sentence might internally and subconsciously say, "Well I'm not sure the sales really are that high," or "Weren't they higher?" Or they may say, "I can't imagine. Where is that red line? I don't know what he's talking about." Maybe they wear a different uniform, or maybe they suddenly become concerned about the fact that they're not in compliance with the uniform.

So, when I'm very specific in my communication, I can actually generate unconscious opposition rather than rapport. Using the principles of the Milton Model, we can communicate the same thing, but with less specificity:

"Imagine what success would be like for you and your team. Where you would be if our sales goals were doubled, and how it might feel to know that you were part of that success?"

"That success? What successes? Sales goal doubled. Where were they at? Where are they going? What it would be like for you and your team? Who's on that team?" It's very non-specific, and so the listener is going to–according to the theory of Milton Erickson–attach the meaning that makes the most sense for me. The listener is going to embrace what it is that we've said.

There are so many techniques that I could teach an entire course just on the Milton Model. One of them is mind reading. For instance, I might say, "I know that you're learning as you experience something new today, reading this book." I know that you are learning. How do I know that? Again, I'm linguistically playing the role of a mind-reader.

Here's another example: "You may wonder if it's okay to have thoughts that are different than others. As we discuss this vision, it is, of course, normal for the mind to think of alternatives—after all, that's what minds do; they create." So, I'm mindreading that they might wonder if it's okay.

Here is another example of mind-reading is: "You're curious to discover how you can be part of this project." I'm presupposing in my mind-reading, and by doing so it is easy for me to, at a subconscious level, gain rapport and cooperation from others.

Another strategy in the Milton Model is using adjectives and adverbs that compliment; it tends to gain agreement with the subconscious mind to get buy-in and acceptance of our presuppositions. For example: "People are pleasantly surprised by the incredible capacity to change." Or again, if I were addressing a group of employees, I might say this: "You'll find a pleasant surprise in your ability to easily recall all of the information in the product description catalogue." The two words there that are adjectives and adverbs that compliment: *pleasant* and *easily*.

Another strategy of Milton Erickson is cause and effect. Words like "makes, causes, forces, because, requires"–these words indicate a cause and effect. When I use these linguistically, it creates agreement. So I might say to somebody, "Because you've come here today and set aside time to learn something new, we know that you will be successful at…" fill in the blank: sweeping the floor, or selling the product, or organizing the community.

Another example: "You've increased your sales in the past four weeks, and this makes achieving your goal even easier over the next few weeks." That's really powerful, that sentence. I use the word "makes," and I've given them a suggestion. The suggestion is that they will increase their sales goal over the next few weeks, and it's an awesome tool for motivation.

Here's another example of cause and effect: "Your devotion to this requires you to be successful, and this makes it even easier to persevere without discomfort." I might use that if I'm trying to motivate people to do a task that is difficult, time consuming, or even above the normal call of duty.

All of these linguistic communication strategies can be employed in a way that can quite powerfully assure the outcomes that we desire.

Strategy 5 – Questioning

I've always been intrigued by Peter Drucker's book *The 5 Most Important Questions You will Ever Ask About Your Organization.* These questions are:

- What is our mission?

- Who is our customer?

- What does the customer value?

- What are the results?

- What is our plan?

These questions are great because they lead to solutions. As discussed in the Transderivational Search discussion, they also cause the listener to look inward to see what their role is. When we ask questions, it often communicates to the receiver, "I'm listening to your opinion, and I value you." In fact, the most successful salesmen I know are those who ask questions of the customer rather than those who tell the customer something.

Strategy 6 – Positive Reinforcement

The old saying teaches that you catch more flies with honey than with vinegar. In our communication with other individuals–whether those are lateral relationships or hierarchical relationships–positive reinforcement, rather than negative criticism, is always a more effective tool at motivating individuals and creating successful outcomes.

Strategy 7 – Non-Verbal Congruence

This is really about our paralanguage, as it's called in literature. It's not only about paying attention to proxemics, but also to body language.

In our face, we have over two hundred tiny micro-muscles. Poker players need to learn how to develop a poker face by controlling those tiny muscles' micro-movements, so that they can conceal the "tells." The "tells" are the automatic emotional, non-verbal communications that we often give through those facial expressions. Ideally, in communicating effectively from a non-verbal perspective, we're going to have congruence between the spoken word and the non-verbal communication.

This involves a number of different aspects, including appropriate eye contact; non-shaming, non-sexual touch; and appropriate styles of clothing and uniform. Think about your posture: where are you leaning? That's the direction that the client's attention is going to go.

Strategy 8 – Humor

Levity, humor, a humorous story, or a short joke that's appropriate in the workplace are all tools which can break tension, increase attention, and lead to success in our communication.

Strategy 9 – Simplicity

Like a good new reporter, consider the 5 W's (and the H): Who, What, Why, When, Where, and How. Whenever I need to communicate something to people, I always go back to the 5 W's. That formula is an easy to remember formula which we have all previously learned. It ends the complexity over sharing a vision, asking for tasks to be completed, or communicating in a positive way.

This chapter has focused on Leadership Communication, providing a thumbnail sketch of what makes an effective communicator. We could spend a great deal of additional time studying each of these strategies on their own. Hopefully though, through this short chapter, you've been encouraged to explore some new strategies which can help you be a success in your leadership communication.

Chapter Ten:

Mindfulness

Mindfulness is not a new idea. In fact, the idea of mindfulness—living fully in the present—is a practical approach for decreasing stress and healthy living that's really as old as the ages.

Certainly, it is recognized from the increasingly pop-culture concepts of Buddhism, but every major world religion has recognized the value of mindfulness in problem solving. Jesus in Matthew 6:27 asks a rhetorical question: "Which of you, by being anxious, can add one moment to his lifespan?" Jesus tells us at the end of Matthew 6, "Don't worry about tomorrow, for tomorrow will worry about itself. Each day has enough trouble of its own." These comments really are the essence of mindfulness—staying fully in the present—because in the present, as long as we're always breathing, we're actually okay. I do a lot of work with those who have a fear of flying, and I often tell them, "As long as you are breathing, no matter what else is going on, you're actually okay."

Because mindfulness has become a popular subject for seminars, trainings, and corporate leadership events, as well as a foundation in therapeutic changework impacting psychotherapy, social work, and marriage and family counseling, it's really important to address a couple of things.

First, although world religions, especially Buddhism, are associated with the concept of mindfulness, this is not because mindfulness is an intrinsically religious or spiritual idea. Rather, it's because historically religion has done what the modern era of psychology does. Just as people turn to therapists for help with life now, religion has been where people have gone for explanations and direction in problem-solving. All major religions of the world have recognized that by staying fully engaged in the present rather than ruminating over the past or fearing the future, we can experience serenity, peace, and calm.

The disciplines of leadership training and psychology are actually new academic disciplines. Prior to the growth of psychology in the twentieth century, religion almost always served to answer questions, not only of a metaphysical nature, but also questions about problem-solving and practical living. This tells us that religion or a lack of religion is not a requisite for practicing, developing, or benefiting from mindfulness, even if the historical context for understanding or applying it has come from a variety of world religions.

Second, mindfulness is actually an empirically validated manner of problem-solving in psychology, and it's well-researched as a requisite for developing effective transformational leaders.[42] It's a foundation of emotional and social intelligence and even a strategy for effective communication. Mindfulness allows us to experience the world as it is, not as it was or as it should be, and this level of acceptance of the present allows us a perceptual position that's really ideal for effective leadership. Mindfulness also gives leaders a vantage point for assessing current strengths and resources based on a present awareness and aligns community members within an organization towards a common and shared experience.

I'm going to share with you a few examples from the academic literature of the value of mindfulness as a strategy in leadership. In a study of nursing leadership, a four-week training program in mindfulness significantly reduced stress levels.[43]

Sauer and Kohls defined mindfulness as, "Being open, present, and receptive to what is happening from one moment to the next without cognitively evaluating the given state or situation." They go on to ask the question, "Can mindfulness significantly contribute to leadership performance?" Essentially their question is this: Does being a mindful person enhance a leader's business success? Their answer is a thoughtful *yes*, based on many factors of understanding mindfulness in the context of leadership.[44]

---

42   Niko Kohls and Sebastian Sauer, "Mindfulness in Leadership: Does Being Mindful Enhance Leaders' Business Success?," in *Culture and Neural Frames of Cognition and Communication On Thinking* (Springer, 2011).

43   T. B. Pipe et al., "Nurse Leader Mindfulness Meditation Program for Stress Management: A Randomized Controlled Trial," *J Nurs Adm* 39, no. 3 (2009).

44   Kohls and Sauer.

Dr. Ellen Langer from Harvard University writes, "In more than 30 years of research, we've found that increasing mindfulness increases charisma and productivity, decreases burnouts and accidents, and increases creativity, attention, positive affect, health, and even longevity." She states that, "Noticing puts us in the present, makes us sensitive to context and aware of change and uncertainty." And she contrasts this with mindlessness, which she characterizes as, "Not good for any organization."[45]

Now, what exactly is mindfulness? I've shared some definitions from various authors, but I'm going to share with you the definition that I use with my clients in counseling. Almost every client who comes to see me has a variety of different issues. They may be interpersonal. They may be emotional. They may be vocational. All of the clients who come to see me, though, come because they want help solving a problem, and with probably 95 percent of the clients, the first strategy I teach them for problem-solving is to stay in the present.

And so, often probably within the first 30 to 40 minutes of my very first session with the vast majority of my clients, I teach them a strategy for practicing mindfulness. In fact, I'm going to share that strategy with you in a few minutes.

But what is mindfulness?

The definition that I give to my clients is this:

Mindfulness is the art and practice of paying attention to this moment. In this moment regrets have slipped away and anxiety about the future is not present. In this exact moment, we're whole, complete, and safe.

Mindfulness in clinical practice and counseling helps a client depart from fear, trauma, impulsivity, and self-defeating thoughts. It's a strategy that I use to train my clients in a new way of experiencing life, thoughts, emotions, and even physical sensations.

This strategy was actually first applied in the clinical context at the University of Massachusetts General Hospital by a gentleman named Jon Kabat-Zinn within the context of pain control. He was working with clients whose chronic pain did not respond to surgery, medical intervention, or medication. Yet he found that even with the presence of very real pain, clients were able to

---

45   Ellen Langer, "A Call for Mindful Leadership" http://www.ellenlanger.com/blog/144/a-call-for-mindful-leadership (accessed March 8 2014).

stay fully focused on the present, learn the strategies of being gentle to themselves, and learn the strategies of not following thoughts, choosing instead to simply let a thought just be a thought. Those clients, even pain control clients, were able to experience a state of wellness.

One of the keys to mindfulness is paying attention with a nonjudgmental awareness to this moment. What that means is that rather than deciding *this thought is good* or *this thought is bad* or *that feeling is good* or *that feeling is bad* or *that emotion is good or bad*, you are simply present with that state. The result of mindfulness training helps people to let go of past hurts or a focus on the past. This is particularly important within a team that's being developed within an organization, again, whether it's a nonprofit or a business or even a family.

Mindfulness helps by decreasing anxiety about the future, fostering awareness of the present, and altering automatic behaviors. Many of our behaviors are subconscious in nature. By being focused on the present, we alter the automatic behaviors, especially those that are self-defeating, that we may have practiced over a period of time. The result of mindfulness training is to help people self-regulate feelings, sensations, and emotions; research shows it's actually a great tool for releasing depression, anxiety, and anger.

Another way to understand mindfulness is to understand the words of the Great Master Oogway. Now, whenever I share this quote people often think, "I've heard that name, the Great Master Oogway. Who is that?" For those of you who have not seen the movie *Kung Fu Panda* in a long time, the Great Master Oogway of course was the turtle who taught the Kung Fu Panda how to do kung fu. In that movie, Master Oogway said, "Yesterday is history. Tomorrow is a mystery. But today is a gift. That is why it is called the present." Now, in reality I've come to learn that it actually wasn't the great Master Oogway who said that first. Some say it was actually Eleanor Roosevelt, our former first lady, who said that first, while others attribute it to Bill Keane, the cartoonist who drew *Family Circus*. In the era of the current culture, the quote is most often attributed to the movie *Kung Fu Panda*.

Probably one of the most effective ways to understand mindfulness is to simply take a moment and practice mindfulness, and so I'm going to guide you through the same simple process that I use with my clients. Read through the instructions and then take a few moments to practice:

Find a comfortable place where you can take a few minutes to really focus on the present. Adjust yourself in the chair so that you're comfortable. Turn off your phone; maybe even close the door and hang a "Do Not Disturb" sign on the door. As you sit comfortably in the chair, close the eyes and pay attention to the breath.

Of course, we've been breathing since the first day of life, and we'll continue to breathe through the end of life, and so the breath is very familiar to us, so familiar that we often don't take time in life to really notice the breath. Over the next few minutes as you breathe in and breathe out, we're going to practice noting the breath, mindfully paying attention to the process of breathing, the feeling of breathing, and the moment of each breath.

Sometimes people ask me, "How long is a moment?" Probably the best answer I can give is "Right now," or "This breath." As you breathe in and breathe out, you don't need to speed up or slow down the breath. There's not really a right way or a wrong way to experience the breath. This is not yoga. This isn't even a time of meditation. It's simply a time of paying attention to the breath. And when you breathe in, notice where the air enters the nostrils and follow the air as you draw it in. Notice the feeling of the flow of the air, the temperature of the air, and the process of breathing in, and as you breathe, follow the breath as it travels from your face through your throat and into your lungs and notice what the breath feels like in your lungs.

There comes of course a point where the breath turns around inside of the lungs, like a swimmer at the end of an Olympic pool, and it becomes an exhale. Notice that point and follow the breath out, noticing the speed and pressure of the air as you exhale. Notice the feeling of the air, even the temperature of the air. As you breathe in and breathe out, this is, of course, just a breath—but it's something we rarely pay close attention to, and so practice paying attention to the breath right now, every aspect of the breath as you breathe in and breathe out.

As you breathe you might also notice other sensations in other parts of the body—an itch or a discomfort—or maybe you'll notice a thought in your mind, your mind wandering. You don't need to suppress those *thoughts. The idea is not even to clear those thoughts. The idea is when you notice those thoughts, sensations, or feelings, to be nonjudgmental of them. Rather than attaching meaning to them and saying this is good or bad, just note that you have the thought, the feeling, or the sensation, and use it as a cue or an indicator to bring your attention back to the breath. You can even say to yourself, "Well, that's a thought. That means I should return back to my breath." By practicing returning back to the breath we are staying in the present rather than following that thought into the future.*

As you breathe in and breathe out, use the breath as a focal point to always return your attention to this moment. Life is composed of a series of moments, each timed with a breath, and by noting the breath, we notice this moment, and you'll notice that as long as you're breathing, you're actually okay. If we live fully in the present, we're able to enjoy the present and maximize our connection to this place, this time, this chair, and these learnings.

Now, that's a basic practice of mindfulness so with the next breath just breathe in and open the eyes, feeling absolutely fantastic from taking a minute in the learning process to really focus on the present.

Chances are pretty good before you started reading this chapter, you had other work and other things you were doing. Chances are pretty good after you are done reading, there are other things that you need to be doing and will be doing. It is so easy for us to spend our time either ruminating or re-experiencing the past or feeling anxious or projecting into the future that we actually miss this moment. Mindfulness is a skill that we are trained in so that through practice paying attention to the moment becomes a new automatic behavior.

Now, during the practice of mindfulness, what should our attitudinal foundation be? There are several elements to this, and first is nonjudgmental, particularly towards ourself or our thoughts. We often judge a thought as a good thought or a bad thought. By judging our thoughts, what we do is we become entangled and engaged in those thoughts. We begin to follow that thought and go through an evaluation process of that thought, apply it to different scenarios and situations, and pretty soon we find ourself projecting outward. By being nonjudgmental and just letting a thought be a thought or a feeling be a feeling, then it is just what it is, and any power that it might hold over us becomes something that we actually have control over.

Practicing mindfulness requires patience. It is a skill that is learned. In my counseling office, I ask my clients to practice mindfulness twice a day each and every day using an mp3 that I give them for a period of 21 days, each and every day for 21 days. The idea here is simple: It takes 21 days to create a new habit. By practicing the new habit, mindfulness, rather than either rumination or anxiety, becomes the new status quo.

Another attitudinal foundation is a beginner's mind. It's really interesting to explore the cognitive processes, the physical processes, and the emotional processes that we experience during a practice of mindfulness and approaching this with a beginner's mind, an open mind, and a willingness to learn something new, even if at first it might seem strange to do. We can truly benefit from practicing and learning mindfulness.

Trust is another attitudinal foundation—trust in the process, trust in ourself, and trust in the value of learning something new. When introducing mindfulness to a piano teacher, one of my colleagues found that the piano teacher said that it wasn't working; he replied, "Did you ever have a student who played Chopin in the first lesson?" Any skill takes time to learn and requires trust in the learning process.

Not striving is the next attitudinal foundation. We don't have to try to be mindful; just be mindful. As Yoda said, "Do or do not. There is no try." Mindfulness leads to acceptance: acceptance of limitations, acceptance of previous experiences in life, acceptance of the inability to control the future. It is, ultimately, a tool not only for staying focused on the present, but also for accessing those resources that are available to us in any particular moment.

And the last attitudinal foundation is letting go. It is sometimes hard not to follow a thought. During a period of silent mindful practice where nobody is guiding you through the process and you are just sitting in silence for a period of two minutes, you practice this by returning your attention back to the breath every time there's a wandering thought, feeling, sensation, or emotion. It takes practice, but it helps us to learn to let go over many different areas of stress.

Mindfulness really is a tool for problem-solving, a separation from pain and suffering. It puts a space in between our emotions and thoughts. It can be a time-out in a busy, stressful day, and it can also help us to avoid anticipatory fear and panic over financial results, the behaviors of others, or even whether or not we have the ability to truly transform as leaders. Mindfulness is a tool for problem-solving because it helps us to alter automatic responses and behaviors that in the past even involved rumination, regret, anxiety, or projection.

This is a short introduction to a topic that has been discussed in lengthy volumes. What I hope is that you found this orientation to the art of mindfulness helpful. Many leadership training programs are focusing on teaching the core skills of mindfulness in a structured way. Any time you have an opportunity over the next couple of weeks or months to increase your knowledge in this area of mindfulness, you will find that it helps you with almost every area of transformational leadership that I've discussed in this book so far, including social intelligence, emotional intelligence, communication, and even in being still and defining your calling.

APPENDIX A:

Nongard Assessment of Primary Representational Systems

UNDERSTANDING
The Nongard Assessment of Primary Representational Systems

Use the following quiz to find out if your client is operating primarily from a visual, auditory or kinesthetic representational system.

Instruct the client to read each statement and consider the 3 responses A, B and C. Have them X or √ the response that most closely matches their thoughts on the subject of the question.

Once complete, you will add up the number of A answers = _____ the B answers = _____ and C answers = _____. If the majority of the answers are A, their representational system is primarily Visual. If most are B, they are primarily Auditory, and if C, they are primarily Kinesthetic.

Of course, all people can access and use all representational systems, but we can usually identify the strongest.

This is information can be very valuable to you. For example, if you are trying to communicate or create a new induction for a new client, knowing their style can help guide the development of an induction that utilizes visualization, or auditory triggers, or feelings, to increase effectiveness. Matching representational systems of our clients is an effective tool for building rapport and overcoming resistance.

1.) When you are injured, what is your immediate response:
____ a.) See the wound as if it is magnified.
____ b.) Hear the sound of impact.
____ c.) Feel the sensation of pain.

2.) When you spell a new or difficult word, do you:
____ a.) Visualize it on a blackboard.
____ b.) Sound it out.
____ c.) Start writing it out.

3.) When you read, do you:
____ a.) See images of what you are reading.
____ b.) Have conversations with the characters.
____ c.) Seek stories with action and behavior.

4.) When you think, do you:
____ a.) Imagine your thoughts as a movie.
____ b.) Hear yourself talking to yourself.
____ c.) Become distracted by external activity.

5.) When driving, do you:
____ a.) Daydream in pictures.
____ b.) Listen to talk radio.
____ c.) Rock out and dance.

6.) If you buy an assemble-it-yourself project, what do you do:
____ a.) Look at the picture on the box.
____ b.) Read the directions out loud.
____ c.) Just start building and complete it by trial and error.

7.) Which is more appealing or interesting to you:
____ a.) Artful images of beautiful people.
____ b.) The sounds of a sensual voice speaking.
____ c.) The feeling of human touch.

8.) When you go to movies or watch TV, do you:
____ a.) Prefer rich scenery of distant places.
____ b.) Enjoy the dialog of heavy movies like court dramas.
____ c.) Get bored and wish you could go do something else.

9.) When you give a speech, do you:
____ a.) Talk with your hands.
____ b.) Hear yourself telling you what to say.
____ c.) Speak slower than other people.

10.) When relating to others, do you:
____ a.) Imagine them taller, fatter, further, closer, or different in any way; or pay particular attention to unusual features they possess.
____ b.) Find it easy to follow the stories, jokes and conversations with others without feeling lost.
____ c.) Move toward them, feeling their energy.

Add up the number of A answers = _____ the B answers = _____ and C answers = _____.

APPENDIX B:
Nongard Strengths and Resources Inventory

NSRI - Nongard
Strengths and Resources Inventory

Copyright © 2014, Richard Nongard.

Name: _____

Date: _____

ID #: _____

1/PUT Make a mark next to any and all of the following that you possess or have access to:

- ☐ Close friend
- ☐ Reliable transportation
- ☐ Pet
- ☐ Internet access
- ☐ Stable living environment
- ☐ Uniforms and clothing
- ☐ Healthy food sources
- ☐ Primary care physician
- ☐ Source of income

2/ISO Make a mark next to any and all of the following that apply to you:

- ☐ Can solve problems
- ☐ Can follow directions
- ☐ Can give clear directions
- ☐ Can work well in team
- ☐ Can work well independently
- ☐ Can listen well
- ☐ Can express thoughts or feelings
- ☐ Can create plans
- ☐ Can develop creative options

3/EJS Make a mark next to any and all of the following items that you have or can do:

- ☐ High school diploma or G.E.D.
- ☐ Military training
- ☐ Vocational or technical certificate
- ☐ College degree or higher
- ☐ Resume
- ☐ Management or supervisory experience
- ☐ Volunteer or charity work
- ☐ Job history more then 6 months
- ☐ Job history more than 2 years
- ☐ Can pass alcohol or drug screenings
- ☐ Able to use typical business communication skills
- ☐ Appropriate attire
- ☐ Able to learn new skills easily

4/PAA Read this list of 24 items before marking any spot. Then mark the 6 items that you think best describe you:

- ☐ Creative
- ☐ Curious
- ☐ Open-minded
- ☐ Inquisitive
- ☐ Wise
- ☐ Brave
- ☐ Persistent
- ☐ Honest
- ☐ High energy
- ☐ Loving
- ☐ Kind
- ☐ Aware
- ☐ Team player
- ☐ Fair
- ☐ Leader
- ☐ Forgiving
- ☐ Humility
- ☐ Careful
- ☐ Impulse control
- ☐ Appreciative
- ☐ Grateful
- ☐ Optimistic
- ☐ Humor
- ☐ Spiritual

5/PIA Read the list first. Then mark 4 of the following which best describe your interests or abilities:

- ☐ Cooking
- ☐ Playing sports
- ☐ Exercise
- ☐ Building things
- ☐ Music
- ☐ Arts and crafts
- ☐ Games and puzzles
- ☐ Singing
- ☐ Reading
- ☐ Writing stories or poems
- ☐ Dancing
- ☐ Travel
- ☐ Family time
- ☐ Community involvement
- ☐ Religious services

6/SSS Make a mark next to any and all of the following who you think are willing to help you at this time:

- ☐ Mother
- ☐ Father
- ☐ Sister
- ☐ Brother
- ☐ Step-parent
- ☐ Grandparent
- ☐ Other relative
- ☐ Best friend
- ☐ Close friend
- ☐ New friends
- ☐ Boss or supervisor
- ☐ Co-worker
- ☐ Religious leader
- ☐ Neighbor
- ☐ Support group
- ☐ Mentor
- ☐ Coach
- ☐ Counselor or therapist
- ☐ Spouse
- ☐ Medical professional

BIBLIOGRAPHY

"Howard Gardner's Multiple Intelligences Theory", Public Boradcasting Service http://www.pbs.org/wnet/gperf/education/ed_mi_overview.html (accessed March 8, 2014).

"Transformational Leadership", Wikipedia.org http://en.wikipedia.org/wiki/Transformational_leadership (accessed March 8 2014).

Aarons, G. A. "Transformational and Transactional Leadership: Association with Attitudes toward Evidence-Based Practice." *Psychiatr Serv* 57, no. 8 (2006): 1162-9.

Antonakis, John, Bruce Avolio and Nagaraj Sivasibramaniam. "Context and Leadership: An Examination of the Nine-Factor Full-Range Leadership Theory Using the Multifactor Leadership Questionnaire." *The Leadership Quarterly* 14, (2003): 261-295.

Bass, Bernard M. and Bruce Avolio, "The Benchmark Measure for Transformational Leadership" http://www.mindgarden.com/products/mlq.htm#overview (accessed March 8, 2014).

Bass, Bernard M., Ruth Bass and Bernard M. Bass. *The Bass Handbook of Leadership: Theory, Research, and Managerial Applications*. 4th ed. New York: Free Press, 2008.

Bass, Bernard M. and Ronald E. Riggio. *Transformational Leadership*. 2nd ed. Mahwah, N.J.: L. Erlbaum Associates, 2006.

Bolles, Mark Emery, Richard Nelson Bolles and Mark Bolles. *What Color Is Your Parachute?: Guide to Job-Hunting Online*. 6th ed. Berkeley: Ten Speed Press, 2011.

Burns, James MacGregor. *Leadership*. 1st ed. New York: Harper & Row, 1978.

Cherniss, Cary, Melissa Extein, Daniel Goleman and Roger Weissberg. "Emotional Intelligence: What Does the Research Really Indicate?" *Educational Psychologist* 41, no. 4 (2006): 239-245.

Conger, Jay Alden and Beth Benjamin. *Building Leaders: How Successful Companies Develop the Next Generation.* 1st ed. The Jossey-Bass Business & Management Series. San Francisco: Jossey-Bass, 1999.

Dobbs, Randy. *Transformational Leadership: A Blueprint for Real Organizational Change.* 1st ed. L, Ar: Parkhurst Brothers Inc., Publishers, 2010.

Dvir, Taly, Dov Eden, Bruce Avolio and Boas Shamir. "Impact of Transformational Leadership on Follower Development and Performance: A Field Experiment." *Academy of Management journal* 45, no. 4 (2002): 735-744.

Goleman, Daniel. *Social Intelligence: The New Science of Human Relationships.* New York: Bantam Books, 2006.

Grice, H. P. *Studies in the Way of Words.* Cambridge, Mass.: Harvard University Press, 1989.

Judge, T. A., A. E. Colbert and R. Ilies. "Intelligence and Leadership: A Quantitative Review and Test of Theoretical Propositions." *J Appl Psychol* 89, no. 3 (2004): 542-52.

Kirkbride, Paul. "Developing Transformational Leaders: The Full Range Leadership Model in Action." *Industrial and Commercial Training* 38, no. 1 (2006): 23-32.

Koh, William, Richard Steers and James Terborg. "The Effects of Transformational Leadership on Teacher Attitudes and Student Performance in Singapore." *Journal of Organizational Behavior* 16, no. 4 (1995): 319-333.

Kohls, Niko and Sebastian Sauer. "Mindfulness in Leadership: Does Being Mindful Enhance Leaders' Business Success?" In *Culture and Neural Frames of Cognition and Communication*

On Thinking: Springer, 2011.

Langer, Ellen, "A Call for Mindful Leadership" http://www.ellenlanger.com/blog/144/a-call-for-mindful-leadership (accessed March 8 2014).

Marshall, Elaine Sorensen and Elaine S. Marshall. *Transformational Leadership in Nursing: From Expert Clinician to Influential Leader.* New York, NY: Springer, 2011.

Maxwell, John C. *Developing the Leaders around You.* Nashville, Tenn.: T. Nelson, 1995.

Mayer, John, Peter Salovey and David Caruso. "Emotional Intelligence: Theory, Findings, and Implications." *Psychological Inquiry* 15, no. 3 (2004): 197-215.

Meisler, Galit and Eran Vigoda-Gadot. "Perceived Organizational Politics, Emotional Intelligence and Work Outcomes: Empirical Exploration of Direct and Indirect Effects." *Personnel Review* 43, no. 1 (2014): 116-135.

Nongard, Richard. *Contextual Psychology: Integrating Mindfulness-Based Approaches into Effective Therapy.* Scottsdale, AZ: Peachtree Professional Education, Inc., 2014.

Pipe, T. B., J. J. Bortz, A. Dueck, D. Pendergast, V. Buchda and J. Summers. "Nurse Leader Mindfulness Meditation Program for Stress Management: A Randomized Controlled Trial." *J Nurs Adm* 39, no. 3 (2009): 130-7.

PracticeWhatUWant. 2013. "From Struggle Comes Success -- Inspirational Video," From Struggle Comes Success -- Inspirational Video.

Rath, Tom. *Strenghts Finder 2.0.* New York, NY: Gallup Press, 2007.

Rosenbloom, Stephanie, The New York Times http://www.nytimes.com/2006/11/16/fashion/16space.html?8dpc=&_r=2&oref=slogin&pagewanted=print& (accessed March 8 2014).

Sjöberg, Sofia "What Do We Know About Traits Predicting Leader Emergence and Leader

Effectiveness?" In *Frontiers in Leadership Research*: Karolinska Institutet

Sutton, Robert, "Hierarchy Is Good. Hierarchy Is Essential. And Less Isn't Always Better" http://blogs.parc.com/blog/2014/02/hierarchy-is-good-hierarchy-is-essential-and-less-isnt-always-better/ (accessed March 8, 2014).

Tourish, Dennis and Naheed Vatcha. "Charismatic Leadership and Corporate Cultism at Enron: The Elimination of Dissent, the Promotion of Conformity and Organizational Collapse." *Leadership* 1, no. 4 (2005): 455-480.

Warren, Richard. *The Purpose Driven Life: What on Earth Am I Here For?* Expanded ed. Grand Rapids, Mich.: Zondervan, 2012.

Webb, Jonice. BellaOnline.

Weberg, D. "Transformational Leadership and Staff Retention: An Evidence Review with Implications for Healthcare Systems." *Nurs Adm Q* 34, no. 3 (2010): 246-58.